The Groupwork Toolkit

How to convert your one to one advice skills to work with groups

Ann Reynolds and Julie Cooper

ISBN 978-0-9559680-1-3

Published by Careertrain Publishing
www.springpublishing.co.uk

info@careertrain.net

Printed and bound in Great Britain.

Contents

Foreword

Is this book for you?

Are you an adviser working one to one providing information, advice or guidance?

Do you now need to work with clients or students in groups?

Are you concerned about converting your skills and working in a different way?

This book is a practical guide to group work, written principally for those who work one to one with clients, providing "IAG" (Information, Advice and Guidance for Learning and Work). It has been written mostly from the perspective of advisers working with adults, but it includes plenty of ideas for groupwork with young people too. In fact, the tools and techniques in this book should help advisers in any sector to develop skill and confidence in working with groups.

There are several reasons why you may need to start providing information, advice or guidance through groupwork rather than one to one. One reason is economic – it seems logical to suppose that it is more cost effective to put over the same information or advice to six people at a time than to explain it six times over to one person.

It is also true that clients can actually gain more from learning some skills and ideas in a group than they can one to one. For some, there is safety in numbers. For others, it is fun to engage in group activities. Everyone will develop their social skills by working collaboratively, taking turns and supporting each other.

However, you may have chosen to be an adviser because you prefer to work one to one, in which case the prospect of leading group sessions may seem very daunting.

This book aims to look group work full in the face and take away the fear, by giving you structures, techniques and ideas to design, plan and deliver sessions that learners benefit from and enjoy. It does not claim to be an academic work offering new models or theories. It brings together techniques and ideas we have found useful, most of which were first developed by other people. You will find in the bibliography a list of the works written by the authors we mention in the text, so if you want to read more detail, you can look them up there.

We offer you a toolkit of user-friendly concepts to help you on your way, giving you food for thought and fresh ideas We hope you will pick those that appeal to you and that you'll enjoy experimenting with them, in your quest to do your very best for all your clients. Once you have seen people enjoy your sessions, you will begin to enjoy them too. We hope this book will light a spark so that you look forward to your sessions and your learners come away buzzing with enthusiasm.

Who are Julie and Ann?

We are independent guidance advisers and trainers who first met in Cambridgeshire when we worked for the county's Adult Guidance Service. We went our separate ways until we met up again a few years ago and decided to join forces to form CareerTrain.

Why we wrote this book

Ann:

One to one always felt right for me. Some of my friends chose careers in teaching but the thought of standing up in front of a class filled me with horror. When I learned about the role of a careers adviser, it seemed ideal.

Then I found that careers advisers had to work with groups too. Help! It's one thing to respond to an individual's needs but when everyone is looking to me to lead the session, how would I cope? Doubting myself, I fulfilled my own prophecy and delivered a number of very dull and uninspiring sessions to groups of unfortunate 15 year-olds.

It was at Peterborough Regional College that I finally saw the light. Faced with a contract to offer group guidance to adults, I decided to enrol on their City and Guilds 730 course (equivalent to the current PTLLS and CTLLS). I learned how to identify course aims and objectives, design activities to suit all types, structure and pace the session, plan and stick to time, keep everyone involved and, crucially, leave people feeling that that they had learned something useful and enjoyed themselves at the same time.

I learned to value my own style, and that gave me the confidence to experiment outside my natural comfort zone. People of my personality type (introvert) and learning style (reflective) are not natural performers. I came to see that our strengths - listening, thinking things through, foreseeing pitfalls, providing depth – are just as important in delivering learning. I found that I could deliver an interesting presentation without needing to be a performer all the time; I could harness the group's energy and let them do the work. I began to find myself less tired at the end of a day's group work than I would be after a day of one to one sessions.

Although things can and still do go wrong – I will share some of my mishaps with you in this book – I have come to really enjoy working with groups. I often choose groupwork now rather than one to one, for all the fun of the lively interactions and the obvious enjoyment the participants get from working together under my guidance and facilitation.

While there's nothing to beat hands-on practice, I believe there are many techniques that you can learn from a book. Julie and I aim to build on the success of our "One to One Toolkit" and share our experience with other advisers who need and want to get the most out of working with groups.

Julie:

My experience is the reverse of Ann's – I began teaching adults many years before I moved into one to one work. Running evening classes in Kent when I had small children led to the City and Guilds 730. Like Ann, I found it to be a very positive experience, and the theories introduced have stayed with me. I always enjoyed the buzz of a group of learners, seeing the pennies drop and the 'light bulb' moments.

Even then, I was curious about how and why people made their choices when they enrolled. I remember suggesting to my boss that we provide a course that was essentially a range of practical tasters for different courses to help students identify which subjects would suit their interests best. Relocating to Cambridgeshire, I took a job in Educational Guidance - advising adults on the best course options to meet their needs. We often ran short courses to help adults prepare for returning to work, brush up job search skills, or decide on a career path. This can be very rewarding work; you will understand why when we look at some of the theory around why and how people learn.

I very quickly discovered that participants often learned as much, if not more, from each other as they did from me. Sometimes a peer has much more influence than the person standing up at the front! Also group dynamics can be so much more powerful than dialogue between two people. In a one to one situation, there is only one voice to encourage and support the client. In a group of peers, the synergy and motivation of sharing experiences and mutual support can, at times, be amazing.

At this stage, giving guidance or advice to individuals was new to me. My job evolved as Educational Guidance became part of the Careers Service locally, and my training involved both an academic qualification and the then brand new NVQ in Advice and Guidance. Many years down the line, like Ann, I take pleasure in both working with individuals and with groups and can't imagine doing either exclusively. We hope you come to enjoy groupwork too, and that we can smooth your path along the way.

Part One
Transferring Your Skills

Let's begin by considering the work you do as an adviser, and think about how you can use the skills you have in the context of groupwork.

In The One to One Toolkit, we used Bedford's model to help us structure our activities in advice work with individual clients. We will review each of the seven stages of this model and the skills that you are familiar with here, in order to consider how they are relevant to working with groups instead of one to one.

In case you haven't seen it, Bedford's seven-stage model for one to one work is on the next page.

Out of the seven stages, Bedford identified two areas as critical for success in working one to one - creating a friendly, encouraging atmosphere and identifying clients' needs. Do you think these remain the most critical for groupwork?

Bedford's model for one to one advice sessions:

	1. Create a friendly, encouraging atmosphere
	2. Establish the broad purpose of the interview
	3. Gather information from the client
	4. Identify the client's needs
	5. Give information to the client
	6. Summarise progress made during the interview
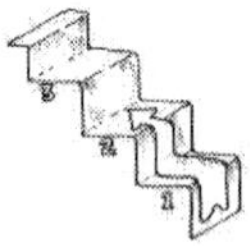	7. Clarify the next steps to be taken

1. Create a friendly, encouraging atmosphere

How does it feel to join a group session if you.....

- have been out of the workplace for some years?
- didn't do well at school?
- don't know who else will be there?
- are unsure of your skill, knowledge or ability?
- feel uncomfortable in groups?
- are in a wheelchair?

Creating a friendly, encouraging atmosphere is equally important for groupwork as it is for one to one work, although you may have to review how you achieve it. The obvious concern, which is a theme that we will return to several times, is around meeting the needs of several people at the same time. You have probably been trained to be client centred, adapting your practice to meet the needs of each client. A shift in mind set is necessary to enable you to start thinking about the needs of the group as a whole.

To a large extent, you will still be looking to meet the varying needs of each individual, but do bear in mind that it is not always possible to please all of the people all of the time - there will be occasions when a group member has to put up with you conducting the group to best serve the wishes or needs of the majority, rather than focusing on his or her particular requirements. There will always be a mix of abilities and confidence levels in a group, and compromises will often need to be made. However, when it comes to creating the right atmosphere, the approach is very similar to working one to one.

Your venue – friendly and encouraging?

Firstly, take a fresh look at the venue you are using. How will it feel for the group members as they enter the room? Is it familiar territory for them? Could it be seen as austere, inappropriate or claustrophobic? If it is shabby and untidy, what image will that convey of your organisation and the level of service the group can expect? Is the room safe, warm and comfortable? We've tried to work with adults in a room plastered with posters aimed at young people, in a community lounge with toys piled in every corner and in a smart board room with table so large there's no room to move around it. Depending on who is in your group, the venue may make them feel they are in the wrong place at best, or unwelcome at worst.

ATMOSPHERE

Here are some examples of times when we have struggled with the physical environment affecting the atmosphere of a group:

- Hot and stuffy – the group can't wait to get away, or they fall asleep.

- Glorious chandeliers and heavily beamed walls and ceilings – in a golf club! There was a twofold problem here – firstly, the light wasn't good enough to read without eyestrain and secondly, it felt like we should have been having a wedding reception, not working.

- The crèche is next door – it's hard to concentrate when you can hear babies crying, especially if one of them is yours.

- Being given a corner in a huge gym. It just felt odd.

- A classroom with a communal area outside – it was hard for the trainees to ignore their friends making faces through the window.

We need to see the venue through the eyes of our group members, and think how it may impact on their comfort and confidence.

Often we have little choice of venue and have to make do with a room that is far from ideal, but it may be possible to rearrange furniture or make adjustments to improve the space. You will need to arrive in plenty of time to organise the space before the start of your session, so that you are composed and ready to welcome people as they arrive. Some group leaders set the tone by using "Welcome" slides or posters, displays of resources or leaflets, or even music that suits the occasion and gives people an impression of what is in store.

You – friendly and encouraging?

Remember, the biggest contribution to the welcoming atmosphere is you - and first impressions count. If you look composed, organised and friendly, there is every chance that all of the group will be able to respond in kind. Lead by example – if you set the tone by respecting and valuing everyone, you should find the group will follow. If you are feeling apprehensive, try to check your body language for tension or other negative indicators. If the group pick up on your discomfort, it is likely to spread through them like wildfire, and people may interpret your anxious posture as being unfriendly.

An easy way of checking that the room is OK and creating rapport is to ask people: Are they comfortable? Do they want a window opened? etc. If you arrive in plenty of time to set up, you should be able to smile and be relaxed as folk arrive. As an adviser, you will be practised at building rapport, breaking the ice with small talk and so on – all useful skills that you can use as the group begins to arrive.

You may have an attendance list or other paperwork that group members need to complete. This may seem arduous and unlikely to put people at ease, but actually having a simple task to do can relax individuals as the group arrives and settles. Involving them in making name cards or badges is another thing you could do at this early stage.

You will need to be very aware of the importance of keeping people safe in a group setting.

EXCLUDED?

Mary was looking forward to the session on how to have more say in her sheltered housing complex. It was being held off site in the housing association offices.

She has a condition that makes walking more than a few steps very painful, so she always checks that there will be disabled access and that she can park her car near the entrance.

She arrived in good time and found the entrance. The meeting was on the first floor, no problem except that the lift was out of order and an engineer was working on it. She struggled upstairs – she could just manage, and didn't want to make a fuss. Getting into the meeting room she sank exhausted into her seat and tuned her hearing aid to the loop system.

The course leader started the presentation – Mary could barely hear. She raised her hand and was told the system was on and she should tune in her hearing aid. No one checked whether this was working, and again, not wanting to be seen as a nuisance, she did the best she could by watching the visual presentation and straining to hear.

You have most likely already encountered folk who are nervous in a one to one setting – don't under-estimate the shyness or fear that some will experience in groups, particularly if they find themselves among strangers, even more so if they are the only person with a disability, the only man, the youngest (or oldest) by far, or feel themselves to be an outsider in some way. They may be worried about being made a fool of, shown as incompetent, mocked or bullied by peers - even if they try to hide it with bravado! Showing reassurance and understanding are skills you need to transfer to the group setting. You could try encouraging more confident or experienced group members to look after nervous newcomers: this can be a way of sharing the workload, as well as getting folk communicating with each other.

Ice Breakers

Of course, you will need a repertoire of ice breakers and introduction exercises that will help you create the right atmosphere – the goal is to be relaxed and friendly, yet purposeful and focused. There are many books and resources that will give you ideas on how to break the ice. In Part Three we describe a few of the techniques we use.

2. Establish the purpose and boundaries of the session

Purpose – Aims and Objectives

In one to one work, most advisers have plenty of experience of establishing the purpose of an interview, and checking that it meets the client's needs. This is generally known as contracting. There are many ways of doing this - everyone has their own style and approach. A popular approach is for the adviser to ask the client what they are hoping for from the session, saying something like "What brings you here today?" and then go on to clarify what they can provide.

You have probably already discovered that good contracting is a very important factor in keeping focus and purpose in one to one work. The same is true of working with groups: it is crucial to establish very quickly the aims and objectives of the session, so that the participants recognise its usefulness for them. If they don't see the value of the session, they are unlikely to participate with enthusiasm.

However, there are some critical differences between contracting with individuals and contracting with groups. In group work:

- You may need to be more directive about the content of the session, and how it will run, rather than allowing an individual to suggest topics for discussion or how to proceed.
- You probably have a clear remit on what you need to deliver in your session, which you will have planned in advance.
- If group members have chosen to attend, the contract has to some extent started before they enter the room. They will have expectations and it is important to make sure you clarify how far you can meet these.

For these reasons, contracting will be less of a two way process than you are used to. Often group leaders will start by asking the group what they want to get out of the session, which is good practice. If it is a one off event, you are unlikely to be able to spare the time to enter into much debate about this, although you must still find time to check your plans against their expectations. So, with a group that has a learning goal it is much more likely to be a case of:

"Today we're going to be thinking about….."

rather than:

"What would you like to discuss today?"

An exception to this general rule is if you are working with a very informal group of people who feel uncomfortable in formal settings. Then a less planned approach may work better, and you could start by saying who you are and what services you provide, and then asking what they want to talk about.

Even where you are not able to give the group freedom to choose the topic, you may be able to give them some options on how you are going to work together, for example:

"You can either discuss issues in pairs, or work as a whole group. Which would you prefer?"

or

"You can ask questions as you go through, or leave questions until I have presented the information".

If you don't agree the purpose of your session, what could go wrong?

- Individuals, or even the whole group, could have expectations that aren't met, leading to frustration or disappointment.
- You may not get the buy-in necessary for the group to focus and work on tasks together successfully.
- Your reputation or that of your organisation could be tarnished if people feel they have not benefited from the session.

Boundaries - Ground Rules

We establish boundaries in one to one work by explaining what we can and can't offer to the client. This is part of contracting, as is clarifying the part we expect our client to play in the process. We need to contract about these issues in groupwork too, so that boundaries are established.

Drawing up a list of ground rules is one way of doing this, and also of reinforcing the aims of the session. We look in detail at ground rules in Part Three, but basically they should be about topics such as comfort, safety, and productivity. If you have plenty of time, you can discuss with the group in order to agree ground rules, but when time is tight, a practical alternative is to present them with a set, and ask them if they can agree to them, or if they want any changes or additions. This is not so very different from one to one work, where some ground rules (for example, boundaries of confidentiality) are probably non-negotiable, and your main concern is to ensure the client understands them.

If you don't set ground rules, what could go wrong?

- You may have to keep asking participants turn off phones, return to topic and so on, so that you lose the flow and end up with a disjointed session.
- Participants may seem to be pushing the boundaries, when actually they do not know what they are.
- You may have to stop to negotiate how members treat each other, if no norms have been established by the whole group.

3. Gather information about clients

What do you need to know?

Now that the group feels welcome and relaxed, and you have agreed the objectives and boundaries of the session, you are ready to get down to the business of the day. Bedford identifies gathering information from the client as the next step in a helpful one to one interaction. We are not talking here about taking names and contact details, hopefully you will have already covered this. Gathering information in one to one work means gaining an understanding of the individual's circumstances, abilities, feelings, constraints and experience in order to give you as full a picture possible of the person in front of you that will help you meet their needs.

Now, herein lies a danger if you are an experienced adviser. It is likely that you are very adept at gathering information from an individual on a one to one basis, by asking questions and being genuinely interested in the client's situation. This probably takes up a fair proportion of the time, but is necessary to ensure that you continue the conversation in a client centred way – putting their needs and interests first.

You may find the going gets tough if you try to do the same in a group situation. It is rarely possible to gather the same amount and depth of information as you would working one to one – and even if you did, you could end up with as many different ways forward as there are people in the group. Would the rest of the group want to hear this level of information about each other or have others know their intimate concerns?

On the other hand, there are benefits to encouraging the sharing of information. Individuals often feel isolated and that they are the only ones facing a particular problem, when in fact the reverse is true – others in the group have the same or similar hopes and dreams. Once this becomes apparent, you will often find that the group takes on a personality of its own, as the group members start to identify with, or empathise with, each other. You can use your one to one skills – showing interest and empathy and intelligent use of questions – to gather information. In addition you will need to use groupwork skills to manage the group and stop any one person dominating; for example keeping to time, dealing with interruptions and staying on topic.

So what information will you be trying to get from your group? It's likely to include:

- Reasons for coming (if they had a choice!)
- What they hope to get out of the session
- Previous knowledge or experience of the subject
- Hopes and fears
- Special individual needs – physical, health, learning needs

We will look in Part Three at ways of getting the group to open up, but for now, think carefully about:

- What do you really need to know in a group setting?
- How you are going to find out?
- How you are going to stop it focusing too much on one member at the expense of others?

THE DOMINATOR

Julie: A long time ago, I was working with a community group. One man, an influential pillar of the local Parish Council, was very vocal in telling me what the group wanted, when and where they could meet and what they expected from me and the organisation I represented.

It took me a while to realise that he didn't represent the views of the majority at all. He just talked the most.

4. Identify the group's needs

The purpose of gathering information from the group is to be able to identify their needs, and here again we encounter the difficulty of a group presenting many different individual needs, possibly conflicting, at the same time.

When you are working with one person, you will identify their needs by using skills such as reflecting back, checking your understanding, assessing and summarising the situation. You can still use these skills in group work, but you'll adapt and use them in a different way.

At first, it will feel awkward to take into account the needs of the group rather than every individual. Try to accept that you will not be able to meet the needs of all the people all of the time. Rather, you will be attempting to satisfy the majority, which on occasion may mean disappointing the individual.

Transparency has its place here. You can be open about your motives for choosing a course of action, for example:

> *"Most of you want advice on how to write a good CV, but James is stuck on an application form. It seems best if we look at CV's to help most of you. James, is it OK if we talk about your form at coffee time?"*

> *"Shelley says she would prefer just to sit and listen to me, but the rest of you want to move around and discuss things with each other. Shelley, would you mind joining in with the others?"*

So, we can be transparent in explaining why we have chosen an activity or topic as being in the best interests of the group. We may identify other needs, but we might decide to keep our assessment to ourselves rather than share it with the group.

What we are saying here is that there can be some negotiation around identifying and meeting needs if – and only if – you feel confident and equipped to deviate from the programme you have planned. If you are already at the limit of your competence by delivering the programme you have planned, you could do more harm than good by trying to deliver something you haven't had time to think about or prepare. Do not over extend yourself by trying to deviate. You could tarnish your own reputation, and may do a disservice to your group members, by giving them a second class service.

In addition to the group's wishes regarding what they want to learn or discuss, you must also be aware of the variety of learning needs you will meet in a group, such as:

- Breadth - do they need specific or general information?
- Depth - do they need the basics, or every detail?
- Level - simple or complex activities?
- Ability to cope emotionally
- Attention span
- Learning style
- A health condition or disability that could affect an individual's potential to benefit from the session unless you find a way to include them

In Parts Two and Three we talk about how to teach people with different learning needs and styles, by deciding in advance what everyone in your group ***must*** achieve, what most ***should*** achieve and the maximum they ***could*** achieve.

ON THE LEVEL

Q: Why did the bright, talkative lad on the Job Search Workshop frighten the tutor half to death by putting on a scary, wrinkly mask when her back was turned?

A: Diversion tactics. He hadn't bothered to go to school so was trying to distract her from discovering he had never learned to read and write. There was little wrong with his intelligence, though.

One of the assessments you will be making about your group is their level of ability, so that you can pitch the content appropriately. Often this is easy to gauge, or you will know from the background information you have. One difficulty that has fooled us more than once is that ability is not always linked to education or how articulate someone is. The brightest sparks may be reluctant to do a paper and pen exercise, while the uncommunicative, expressionless person may well thrive on it.

5. Give information to the group

Up to this point it seems that in many ways, your role in groupwork needs to be more directive than in one to one work, because you have a wide range of opinions and personalities to take into account.

When it comes to giving information, however, perhaps on occasion the reverse is true. Often you will still need to be in control of the information you provide, but sometimes it may serve each person's interests better if you encourage and enable them to acquire the information for themselves.

When we provide information in a one to one setting, we usually answer the individual's questions, explaining in language they understand, maybe looking at brochures or websites together. Sometimes we send clients away with information to read, or to do their own research. There is definitely a place in groupwork for this kind of information giving, so you can use the skills you have already developed.

During groupwork, you can provide a range of resources or exercises so that people gain information in a self directed way – each group member can select the information or learning they want from the range available. This is one way you can begin to address the issue of mixed abilities: you can get the measure of your participants by observing which materials they gravitate towards, or how fluently they can discuss what they have discovered.

6. Summarise progress made during the session

Usually in a one to one session, we recap jointly with the client the progress made during the interaction, and record the outcomes on an action plan or client notes. This helps our clients see the road travelled, progress made, and what they need to do next to move in the right direction towards their goals. Sometimes we use techniques like timelines (described in The One to One Toolkit) to help them see their journey and steps along the way.

The important thing in working with groups is to enable people to identify what they have learned and how they have developed, so that they recognise their own achievements. Far too often people do not see for themselves how they have changed and grown, when it is clear to others around them.

As we said earlier, in a group session you have less flexibility to allow individuals to set the agenda - but you will have set some learning objectives or outcomes for the group session. We will explain how to do this more in Part Three, as it is a very important aspect of groupwork. If you have set objectives, it is easy to revisit them at the end of the session to see whether or not they have been met. This is important because as well as reinforcing what they have learned, it can give the group a sense of achievement.

The end of the session is another time when you can be less directive, and turn the tables so that the group can tell you what they think they have achieved, rather than you telling them. You probably already do ask individuals what they have got out of a one to one session; the same technique is very effective with groups, because hearing what other group members have gained from the session can help inspire and motivate individuals.

The group will find it very rewarding if you can give your own feedback after you have heard from them, perhaps mentioning things like:

> *"You've worked really hard today"*

"It's so nice, the way you supported each other"

"This was not easy but you really seem to have grasped the facts".

It's not viable to do it every time, but where possible and where time permits, we like to make a positive comment about each and every group member for them to take away. A successful group that has gelled well may be able to pitch in at this point and talk about each other, pointing out strengths, progress and good qualities that they have observed in their colleagues. If you can accomplish this, the feel good factor will carry your group members far.

7. Clarify the next steps – the Action Plan

You are unlikely to be able to write individual action plans for every group member. Time simply will not allow it, and then there is the issue of keeping the rest of the group engaged in an activity while you try and get round each individual. Some advisers, coaches and mentors don't write action plans anyway – they give the responsibility back to the individual, who can then take ownership of the process. In a group session, this can be a good policy.

You may advise some potential options for next steps, there may be obvious progression routes, or you may pick up on individual needs that have been identified and suggest ways forward, but it is for the participants to identify the next steps they feel will take them in the right direction.

It depends on the purpose of your group session how diverse the progression routes or next steps may be, so you will choose a method of clarifying the next steps that reflects the ability level and interests of the group members. You may ask them to complete a written exercise as a planned activity during the session - we have used many adaptations of development plans that ask questions like:

- What have you learned today?
- How will you put it into practice?
- What are your action points from today?
- When will you make a start on them?

Even if the exercise is written individually, it can be good to encourage people to share aspects of their action plan with the group (or in pairs or small groups), for the same reasons we suggested sharing needs and concerns: group synergy can be very motivating, and may give them the extra bit of commitment needed to make their plans a reality. When asking people to share their plans, do make sure it is a voluntary activity and give them the option to keep these private if they prefer to.

Groupwork Skills

We've had a brief look at the skills you have as an Adviser, and thought about how they can be transferred to be used in groupwork. Now we are going to turn the tables and consider the skills you need to run a group successfully, so that you can compare them with your existing skills set and identify your own development needs.

The checklist we have come up below with is a very rough guide and of course it could have been longer. You may not be entirely clear what some of the terms mean at this stage but we suggest you treat it as an initial exploration and use it to benchmark your current level of competence. Try to self-assess by giving yourself a score out of ten for each of the skills listed under the four headings we believe make for excellent groupwork:

- Organisational skills
- People skills
- Training skills
- Presentation skills

At the end of the checklist is a Personal Development Plan. You can use it to start thinking how you might address some of the skills gaps you identify.

Most of these topics will be covered in this book, with the exception of some aspects of people skills – we have worked on the assumption that most people reading this will have these skills already. If you want to brush up on people skills or investigate them further, you could refer to the One to One Toolkit.

Group Work Checklist

People Skills	**Self assessment**
Building rapport, ice breaking	
Noticing people's needs and feelings	
Managing relationships between group members	
Boundary setting	
Active listening	
Managing group while valuing individuals	
Negotiating	
Keeping calm	
Sense of humour	
Motivating and encouraging	
Getting people to join in	
Communicating clearly	
Self awareness – own impact on others	
Showing interest and empathy	

Organisational Skills	**Self assessment**
Time (and self) management	
Planning and preparation	
Flexibility and adaptability	
Access to and choosing resources	
Evaluation processes and methods	
Administration, completing paperwork	

Training Skills	Self assessment
Identifying aims and setting learning objectives	
Understanding how people learn	
Repertoire of training methods	
Facilitating	
Explaining clearly	
Handling group dynamics	
Devising activities	
Creating learning materials	
Assessing people's progress	

Presentation Skills	Self assessment
Projecting confidence	
Conveying enthusiasm	
Varying tone of voice	
Ability to hold attention	
Making it relevant to this audience	
Flexibility of delivery	
Subject knowledge and content selection	
Using visual aids, e.g. PowerPoint	

……….Is there anything else you think should be added?

Personal Development Plan

People Skills

Area for Development	How I will achieve it

Organisational Skills

Area for Development	How I will achieve it

Training Skills

Area for Development	How I will achieve it

Presentation Skills

Area for Development	How I will achieve it

Part Two
How People Learn

Your role as an adviser is to help people move forward in their lives. To do this, they may need to learn - new information, new techniques and new ways of looking at a situation. Running a group session can be a very effective way of helping people learn. Before starting to plan and deliver your session, it is worth pausing to reflect on what learning means and what it involves.

Please be assured that you don't need to memorise all the theory that follows before you can start to deliver group sessions. If it suits you better, you can skip straight to the next session about practical planning, and revisit this section when you want to explore models and concepts to underpin your work. You will only find a short introduction to each one here, to whet your appetite. If you want to know in more depth, please look in the bibliography for sources.

In this section we will consider:

What? How? Why?

What?

- What is learning?
- What happens when we learn?
- What is different when it has happened?
- What steps do people go through when they learn?

The answers to these questions will help you organise your learning sessions to achieve maximum results.

We give you a definition of learning and tell you about the Learning Cycle so that you understand the activities people progress through as they learn. The Nine Events of Learning are introduced here, and returned to in Part Three so that you can plan a group experience all the way from motivating people through to assessing what's been achieved and putting it into practice. We also look at the Three Domains of Learning to help you understand how learning occurs in different ways and at different levels.

How?

How do people learn? Does one size fit all? As you know from one-to-one work: No, it doesn't! Different people learn in different ways, and a look at the main learning styles identified by educationists will help you plan and deliver sessions that cater for everyone.

We introduce you to:

- Reinforcement
- Feedback
- Modelling
- Preferred Learning Styles
- Sensory Based Learning Styles
- Mind Styles – Which side of the Brain?
- Aptitude – Ability – Intelligence
    - IQ
    - Multiple intelligences
    - Convergent or Divergent Thinking
- Prior Learning
- Bite Sized Chunks and Avoiding Indigestion
- Learning Curves
- Conscious Competence

Why?

Why do people want to learn? People will gain more from your session if they really want to gain skills or knowledge. So what makes one person keen to learn while another has no interest? In this section we look at how you can tap into their motivation.

Motivation is a huge topic that relates to a lot more besides learning. We'll dip very briefly into some theories to see how they can help us run a successful group session:

- Maslow's Hierarchy of Needs
- Levels of Motivation for Learning
- Pegagogy and Andragogy
- Process
- Ethical, Client centred Groupwork

That was a brief overview – now to the detail of the **What? How?** and **Why?** of learning.

What?

What is Learning?

A definition will help. It is generally accepted that we can define learning with one word:

Change

Learning = Change

If I learn, I am different from how I was before. Maybe I:

- know more
- understand more
- feel differently about something
- can do something new
- can do it more skilfully, quickly, effectively

When you run a group session, your aim is that something will change for your learners.

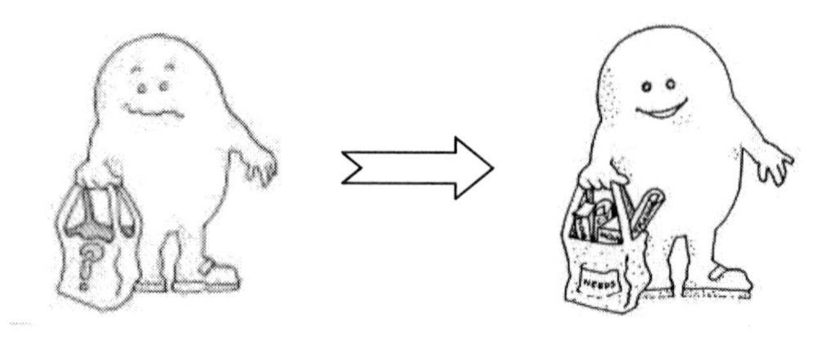

What Happens When We Learn?

The Learning Cycle

Kolb's Learning Cycle (Kolb, 1985), which we have simplified here, shows us the stages we need to go through in order to learn effectively.

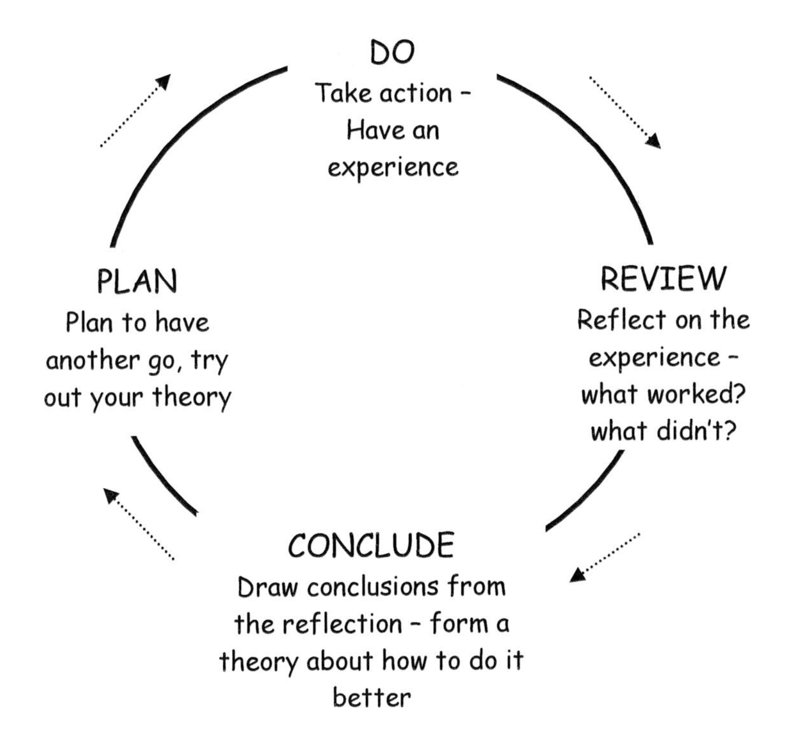

How does this work in practice?

We often start by having an **experience** (for example, we attend an interview and don't get the job). Then we **review** it (I wonder what went wrong? what could I have done differently? what do other people do?). After reflecting (and maybe researching by reading or asking people) we **reach conclusions** (it is advisable to find out more about the job in advance, to dress appropriately, to practise). We then **plan** to put these new ideas into practice next time.

Kolb sees the process as a continuous spiral – the planning stage leads back to having the experience again to try out our plan, and then reflecting on how it worked this time, drawing new conclusions, and so on.

Learning can begin at any stage in the cycle. **Doing -** A small child might touch a hot stove and burn himself – starting with the experience, on which he reflects and concludes that touching a hot stove will hurt and so plans to avoid it in future.

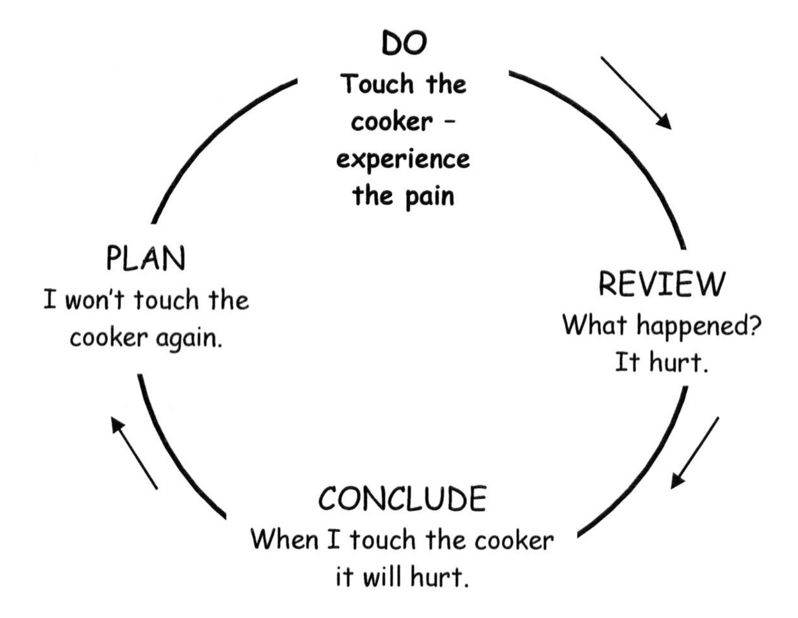

He might, though, have first heard from his mother that it will hurt if he touches the cooker. **Planning -** He might decide to experiment, to test out this theory: so he plans an experience – touch it very quickly just to see if she's right.

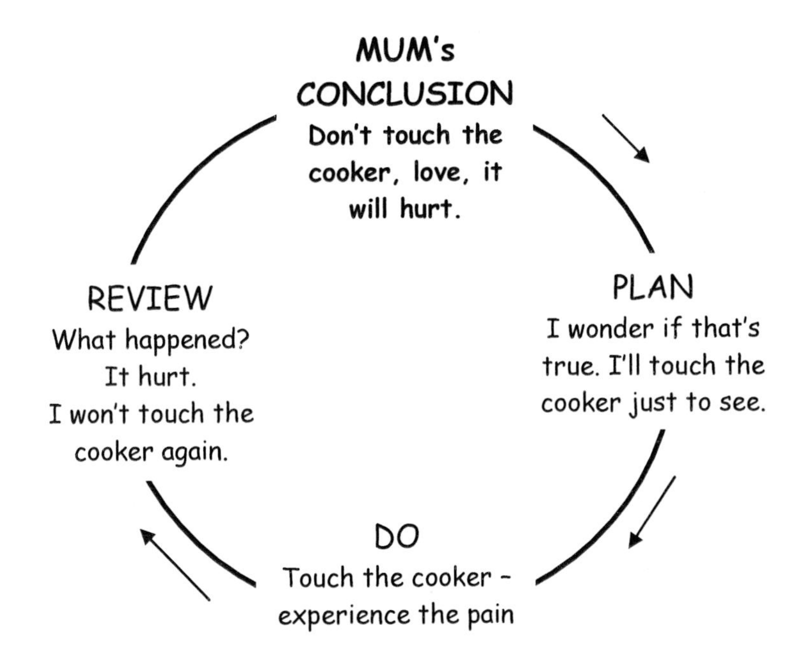

Kolb says the **Conclude** stage can be based on someone else's conclusions as well as our own. When the child planned to touch the cooker, he was prompted by his mother's conclusion "if you touch the cooker, it will burn you". Of course, another child might have accepted his mother's "theory" in the first place and planned to keep away from the cooker from the start. But people often need to experience for themselves before they fully accept what others tell them.

Someone else's conclusions may be presented as a theory. If you were to introduce a theory (as we are doing here) to a group, you can ask them to think abut how it is relevant to their own situation, or how they might plan to apply it in practice. For example, you might tell your group the theory of how to answer an interview question about strengths and weaknesses, and then ask them to plan what they would say about their own abilities. You could then move them on to the experience stage by role playing, and so on.

You may prefer to throw them in at the deep end and make them **do** role play first. For example, you could get them to go into a shop and ask about a job vacancy, without any preparation. Then get them to **reflect** on how well it worked, **plan** how they could improve and have another **go**. Bear in mind, however, that a lot of people hate the idea of role play. Unless you know you are working with very active or very confident learners, it may overwhelm them unless you build up to it more gradually.

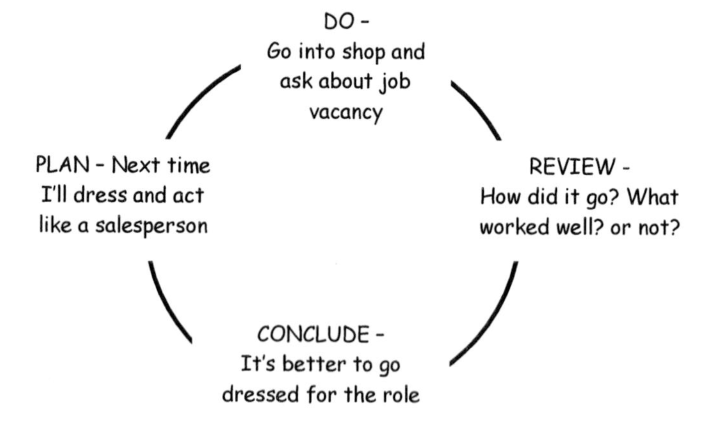

What do ***you*** usually do when you try something new? Act first or think first? Have a go straight away or read the instructions first? Kolb suggests we all learn best by going through all four stages. However, we all tend to prefer one or two of the stages, which can cause us to neglect the others. We will look at this again in Preferred Learning Styles, later in this section. When you plan your session, remember Kolb's learning cycle and plan activities that take your group members through every stage.

The Nine Events of Learning

Have there been times when someone will not take on board what you are trying to tell them? Maybe there are some facts that you just cannot remember, however many times you are told? Some people's names or birthdays, perhaps, or how to programme the central heating, whereas others you will always remember even if you only heard them once?

Gagné (Gagné, 1965) suggested that although some learning happens almost by accident (like the child touching the hot stove), when we plan a groupwork session we cannot just wait and hope people will learn. We need to make sure nine things happen:

1. Gain people's attention
2. Inform them of the objectives (*what you plan to teach them*)
3. Stimulate recall of prior learning (*help them remember what they already know, so they can build on it*)
4. Present stimulus material (*introduce new information*)
5. Provide learner guidance (*help people make sense of the new information and link it to what they know already*)
6. Elicit performance (*give them opportunity to practise*)
7. Provide feedback (*let them know how they're doing*)
8. Assess performance (*if required*)
9. Enhance retention transfer (*make it stick*)

Some of these phrases may be unfamiliar to you, so we have added a few words to try and make them clear. Once understood, they provide a good framework for any learning intervention. We explain them more, with ideas of how you can achieve each one, in Part Three, where we have adapted Gagné's nine events into a six stage structure. You can use this to help plan a session that will take your group step by step through the process.

The Three Domains of Learning

Traditionally, education seemed to be all about knowledge and understanding. If someone knows a lot of facts, they are thought to be clever. They can win quizzes and pass exams.

Knowledge is important in the world of work. I want my careers adviser to know what jobs are available, what the entry requirements are and which colleges offer the training. I want my doctor, my car mechanic or my prime minister to have sufficient knowledge to do their job properly and to achieve results for me.

But can the ability to do a good job be proven by the fact that they have passed exams and know a lot? Think of the teacher who has graduated with first class honours from the most academic university but cannot pass on his knowledge to a group of students.

Bloom (Bloom, 1956) proposed that learning can be divided into three areas, or domains:

- The **Cognitive** domain
- The **Psychomotor** domain
- The **Affective** domain

These may not be familiar words to you. In a nutshell, they mean:

Cognitive	Happens in the brain – thought processes
Psychomotor	Brain plus rest of the body – skill at doing things
Affective	Feelings, emotions, attitudes, beliefs, heart

You may have seen groupwork objectives described in similar terms:

- **Knowledge** Cognitive
- **Skills** Psychomotor
- **Attitude** Affective

Bloom and others break down each of these domains in detail, as activities on a scale, moving from the simplest to more complex levels.

Let's look at them in turn.

Knowing and Thinking – The Cognitive Domain

Cognitive learning is about knowing, but not only about knowing.

- I **know** my 12 times table but what use is that knowledge on its own?
- I **know** that it's important at a job interview to make a good first impression and to give clear examples of my skills, but will that knowledge alone get me the job?

Six Levels of Cognitive Learning

Bloom proposed that cognitive learning moves up through six levels, each using and building on the previous one, showing an increasingly complex set of thinking skills. His ideas have been slightly re-organised (Anderson and Krathwohl, 2001) into the following progression:

Level 1 Remembering (or *knowing*)
Level 2 Understanding
Level 3 Applying
Level 4 Analysing
Level 5 Creating (or *synthesising*)
Level 6 Evaluating

What are your objectives for your group session? The higher the level of cognitive learning, the better you will equip people to succeed in their chosen area. By the end of your session they may **know** what a CV should look like. Of far more lasting use would be the ability to **apply** this knowledge and **create** a range of CV's for themselves, to apply for different jobs in the future.

Here's an example of each level of cognitive activity, based on learning to write a CV.

1. **Know and remember:**
   Fact - It is usual for a CV to be no longer than two pages, and often one page is ideal
   Fact - A CV must include your name, address, telephone number and email address
   Fact - There is no rule that you have to give your date of birth or marital status on a CV

2. **Understand**
   The reason why you need to give your name, address, telephone number and email address is to enable the employer to contact you if they are interested. The reason why you need to keep to one or two pages is that busy employers need to spot the important information quickly – information that will attract them. Understanding the reasons behind the facts will help you decide what else to include or leave out, including your date of birth or marital status. Understanding makes you more independent.

3. **Apply**
   For the learning from the CV workshop to be of any use, you need to be able to apply this knowledge and understanding to your own situation. You need to have a go and create your own CV.

4. **Analyse**
   If you want to make your CV more attractive, it must be tailored to what employers are looking for. You need to (a) analyse what employers want and (b) analyse your own experience to select appropriate information. Now, you can tailor your CV to different jobs – even more useful in your future career.

5. **Create**
   Armed with all these cognitive skills, you are now in a position to create CVs for many different situations, even to break some of the rules you learned as "fact" at the first stage. People who

come up with new solutions to problems are those who move the world forward.

6. **Evaluate**
   If your CV is not working for you, you will want to know whether it's just bad luck or whether you could make changes to improve your chances of being selected for interview.

Is it really possible to take people through all six levels in one groupwork session? Of course, we must be realistic about what can be achieved in the time, but this does not mean you have to limit your objectives to giving knowledge alone. In fact, why gather people together in a room just to pass on facts? You could do that more cost effectively by giving them a book or DVD. Why not use the dynamics of a group environment to help them understand, apply, analyse, create and evaluate?

To keep your objectives realistic within the time available, you might narrow your focus. Rather than covering all aspects of job search, concentrate on just the CV, or even on just the "Profile" section of the CV, but aim to teach not only the facts but also how to apply them analytically and creatively. You can always provide further exercises and information to take away, for those who want to develop further after the session.

Doing – The Psychomotor Domain

The Psychomotor Domain of learning is more practical. It is about doing – using our bodies as well as our minds. Staying on the subject of CV writing, the psychomotor skills required are those that move our fingers across the keyboard (without looking and at speed), and at a more basic level to manipulate a pen or pencil to form letters and write.

Advisers don't deal with psychomotor skills very often. These are more the domain of those teaching crafts or sports – for example, carpentry or yoga. One area of psychomotor skill that IAG advisers could work on with clients is how to present themselves: speech and movement, for example in job interviews.

IAG clients are always asking for more help to prepare for interviews. Cognitive learning alone is only the beginning, and not really what they are worrying about. Advice, an information sheet, a DVD: these are better than nothing, but the group situation provides a brilliant opportunity to get up and move about – practice walking through the door with a smile and the right handshake, sit down without looking clumsy, speak above a whisper without booming at the interviewer – these are examples of psychomotor skills that will empower your learners.

Five Levels of Psychomotor Learning

Bloom's initial work was developed by R H Dave (Dave, 1975) proposing that psychomotor skills develop through five levels:

Level 1	Imitation	(*watch an expert*)
Level 2	Manipulation	(*have a go*)
Level 3	Precision	(*perfect it*)
Level 4	Articulation	(*relative mastery*)
Level 5	Naturalisation	(*second nature*)

To help you plan your psychomotor skills learning session aimed at helping people improve their performance at job interviews, here's an example of each level:

1. **Imitate** – Watch an expert
   To imitate, the beginner must first watch and listen to someone else performing well. Show them a DVD, or demonstrate the skill yourself.

2. **Manipulate** – Have a go
   They must try it out for themselves, having a few attempts and seeing what works best. They could practise walking into the room aiming to look confident and friendly. Video or photograph each person. Another idea would be to give them an interview question, divide them into pairs, each taking turns in asking the question and in responding to it. Ask them to evaluate their own performance and receive feedback from their peer.

3. **Precision** – Perfect it
   Set up further role plays with opportunities for feedback, so that they can do more of what works and less of what did not work. Provide more than one opportunity, so that they can replace a memory of a first bad performance with the knowledge that they can improve.

4. **Articulation** – Use it in the real world
   Finish with a full interview role play for them to put into practice all they have learned. Encourage them to continue practising at future interviews. This will give them a silver lining to the cloud in case they do not succeed at their first interview – it was a good opportunity to practise and hone their skill.

5. **Naturalisation** – it becomes second nature
   Eventually, they will automatically perform better at interviews. You will not reach this stage with them in one group workshop, but you can tell them how psychomotor learning works, to build their resolve to keep trying. There will be the pot of gold at the end of the rainbow!

Feeling And Believing – The Affective Domain

How many of us have missed out on jobs because of our performance at interview? We know all the rules, we've worked out exactly what to do and say, we do an excellent dummy run in the kitchen with our partner. Then we turn up on the day and see the other candidates. The throat constricts, the hands tremble and the butterflies take over, as we think of all the reasons why everyone else has so much more to offer.

It's the same with sport – a player's psychomotor skills can be perfect, but sports psychologists are brought in to make sure that they are not sabotaged by feelings. The tennis player swearing at himself (and others) on the court is paying attention to his feelings. If we don't pay attention to our clients' feelings, most of the other learning we provide may be wasted.

The affective domain is especially relevant for advisers working with clients to help them overcome personal barriers, whether it's about gaining new skills, getting a job, or giving up smoking, alcohol or drugs. Often these barriers are in the client's mind rather than real. Much of our work with clients is focused on changing (learning = change) their feelings, values and beliefs, eg:

Confidence

- in their ability to succeed
- in society – is there a job out there for them?
- in their ability to put on a good performance

Motivation

- to change to a more socially acceptable lifestyle
- to start a course
- to attend college regularly or to keep applying for jobs

Beliefs

- about the rights and wrongs of crime or substance abuse
- about their own value to others
- to feel "I am worth it"

Five Levels of Affective Learning

Can you change values, beliefs and feelings? What makes someone believe that they are "worth it", or decide to give up an unhealthy or anti-social lifestyle? Bloom and colleagues offer a framework of levels in this domain showing how people change their feelings and beliefs. An awareness of these can help you to plan your session and measure its success:

Level 1 Receiving	(*becoming aware of the new value*)
Level 2 Responding	(*having an opinion about it*)
Level 3 Valuing	(*seeing its worth, believing in it*)
Level 4 Organising	(*integrating it into your existing beliefs*)
Level 5 Characterising	(*internalising it as part of your character*)

This all sounds very theoretical – let's apply it to a real life situation of Ann's. Her starting point is the belief that she is hopelessly unfit and incapable of learning anything sporty:

1. **Receiving**
   A few years ago, a new keep fit class was starting in our community centre and some of my friends joined. They seemed to like it and wanted me to go too.

2. **Responding**
   My response was: Exercise is for other people, not me. I've always been useless at sports and I'll look stupid if I try.

3. **Valuing**
   Somehow, my friends persuaded me to go to a session with them. Terrified of making a fool of myself, I hid on the back row. At my first session, the teacher gave us very simple steps to copy and although at first I mostly watched, I began to see that I might be able to do this. I also saw that some of the others were no more slim or graceful than I was, and yet they seemed to be enjoying themselves. Gradually, I realised that I was not going to be judged or commented on, and I joined in more and more until I was really looking forward to the class each week.

4. **Organising**
   I began to look at exercise in a different way and realise that anyone can do it. I reorganised my thinking to see that you did not have to be good at it, this was not the point.

5. **Characterising**
   I now see myself as a reasonably fit and active person, ready to try new and different forms of exercise.

Knowing about affective learning can help you with group work in several areas:

- Motivating and encouraging your group members
- Setting objectives and evaluating your session
- Paying attention to process as well as content in your session

Let's look at these briefly in turn.

Motivating your group

We discuss motivation further on in this section, and you can't ignore it at any stage of your group work, even the planning stage. You need to find out how individuals feel about being at your session and you may need to change their feelings so that they are positive enough to participate, ideally to learn and certainly not to spoil the session for others.

Interview Techniques Workshop

Julie and Ann both learned a lesson recently. We've both had a lot of experience at delivering half-day job interview coaching workshops to adults, usually very successfully. By coincidence, one December, we were each asked to run a workshop on the same topic for 16 year-olds, one in a school and the other for an entry to employment group. Each of us set objectives to deliver the usual content, adapting our course materials to make them appealing to younger people - so we thought.

What we did not take into account was that both groups of young people were a lot more interested in the Christmas holidays and festivities, and did not need to apply for jobs till next summer.

Result: These younger audiences did not engage fully with the session (this is a polite description!).

Their affective learning: That was boring. Work's boring. (Those evaluation forms were painful to read, although we had a good idea what they would say - younger people can be refreshingly honest!)

Setting Learning Objectives

When you set the objectives for your session, will you include the Affective Domain? If people's performance is governed by their feelings as well as by their knowledge and skill, you may want to design certain parts of your session simply to build their confidence and self-belief. You may decide that affective learning alone is a sufficient objective for your session – so long as people feel better at the end, they may not need to have taken on new knowledge or skills.

Process and Content

Process and content go hand in hand and you can't ignore process in any interaction between people. Knowing about affective learning reminds you to pay conscious attention to the process in your session. What does this mean?

Process is about what actually goes on, regardless of what the session is about. However well you plan the content, little can happen if you forget about process. Never under-estimate how easily even confident people can be put off if they feel uncomfortable or excluded.

Car Maintenance Class

Ann, in her early 20's, had just bought her first car, her pride and joy. She wanted to learn a bit about it, so she wouldn't have to ask for help every time something went wrong.

She signed up for "Car maintenance for Beginners" and turned up at the first session. She walked into a room full of middle-aged men. They stared, then carried on with their conversations. The tutor came in and launched straight into a presentation about carburettors. The men asked questions about problems with their own cars. This continued throughout the session. No one spoke to Ann and she couldn't understand a word.

Ann's affective learning: I'm a wimp for not pushing myself forward and asking when I didn't understand. But perhaps I'm stupid for thinking I could learn about cars, it's too hard for me.

Result: Ann didn't go back, wild horses wouldn't drag her there, even to request a refund of the term's fee.

Bingo and chocolate buttons

Ann observed an adviser delivering a session on job families to a group of 16 year-olds from an entry to employment scheme. The session lasted no more than 30 minutes. The adviser delivered her message through a bingo game with chocolate buttons for counters.

Affective learning: the bingo was fun, and we got chocolate. Learning about careers is not totally boring. That adviser's OK.

Result: they were queuing up to book their one to one with her.

As we said, there are times when it is more important to get to know people and keep them amused and comfortable than to impart anything new. You would be surprised how much learning can occur when people are enjoying themselves.

We return to process when we look at the life cycle of the group in Part Four.

How?

How do people learn?

Reinforcement

Behavioural theory (you may have heard of Pavlov and his dog – Pavlov, 1927) tells us we learn through **conditioning**. This means that people learn from the response they get to what they do:

- Child touches the hot cooker – it hurts – he does not do it again.
- Child gives mum a gift – she's happy – he enjoys giving presents.

Behaviourists call this reinforcement, which can be positive (mum's approval and love) or negative (painful burn from the cooker). The lesson here for us is that we can create a situation where the learner will repeat the behaviour we require if we ensure that positive reinforcement (a pleasant consequence) follows the behaviour.

The theory also talks about rewards; in the example above the child has the reward of a happy mum. What rewards could you offer group members to show approval or progress? Showing you are pleased can be a reward in itself – your non verbal behaviour (body language) will display your happiness. Think about verbal rewards (e.g. encouragement, praise, affirmation) and more tangible things like certificates or sweets. In Part Three, we give you some examples of rewards we have used.

Of course, reinforcement can be negative as well as positive. There are times when you want to stop a group member doing something in a certain way. If the issue is behavioural, see our tips in Part Four. If it is about performance, for example they carry out a task the wrong way, you usually need to correct it.

If the performance problem persists, bear in mind that the individual may not understand what is expected, in which case you might have to rethink how to explain the task. Just occasionally, a person who keeps getting it wrong could be enjoying the individual attention they get from needing help.

ENCOURAGING BAD BEHAVIOUR?

Julie: During a group session, one participant who appeared to have a low attention span kept playing games on his mobile phone under the table. I dealt with this by working hard to keep him involved, to distract him from the lure of the phone.

Result? He had far more interaction with me than any other group member. Was this fair? I felt he had been rewarded for his behaviour, and that I had just reinforced that inattention pays.

Feedback

As you have probably realised, feedback is a key way of reinforcing the behaviours or actions that you are looking for. But it has many more uses in helping people develop, and you will not be able to deliver any group learning without providing feedback.

Do you agree with us that...

1. Participants want feedback – if they make the effort to perform or to speak out, they want to know if they have got it right?
2. Every person in your group could be anxious and vulnerable?

3. Everything you do from the start of the session will, whether you intend it or not, provide feedback to your group members?

You need to give feedback, but it is not always easy. So how can you do it well? You may have heard of the ...

Feedback Sandwich!

Compliment
These bits are perfect
That part is particularly good because....

Coach
But this could be improved - Specifically in this way

Encourage
You're making brilliant progress
I really appreciate the effort
you are putting in

Feedback, understandably, is a very sensitive issue. Some will take in their stride, others may get it out of all proportion and take it personally. Some people feel patronised if told they have done well when they know they could improve. Make sure that your feedback is encouraging, uplifting and motivating. This is a very tall order if your protégée just isn't grasping the task in hand. You need to address this – they want to know how to do it properly – but if you remember to use the Feedback Sandwich, you will do a far better job than if you just blurt out their shortcomings. Many of our clients have enough self esteem issues without us adding to them.

TREAD CAREFULLY

A client wanted the adviser to look at her CV, and presented him with a hand drawn bubblegram. He assumed it was a working tool to help her think about what to include, and after a cursory glance at the content, he began to talk about what type of layout might suit her experience.

She burst into tears. She had laboured long and hard, and in her mind she had produced a finished document that she hoped would be the key to a new job. Sometimes we underestimate the time and effort a client or student has put into something, so we seem dismissive.

In this case, the adviser took a step back to the basics, and reviewed with her what she wanted the CV to achieve, who might read it, and what they would be looking for. He realised the importance of acknowledging the work she had done.

Often we are working with people precisely because their lives are not on track. They may not have been in work or education for a long time, which can have an insidious effect on confidence levels. We need to remember that.

It is easy to focus our attention on how we deliver negative feedback, and rightly so – it is important to get it right. But first, for the top layer of your Feedback Sandwich, make sure you have a good repertoire of ways of giving positive feedback. How many ways of saying "Well done!" can you list? We give you some of our ideas in Part Three. Here is a checklist of the main points to bear in mind when giving feedback – they apply in any situation:

- **Acknowledge** the other person's qualities and give positive reinforcement, perhaps by mentioning their strong points or their worth as a group member.
- **Be Supportive** in manner – do not attempt to give critical feedback when feelings are running high, nor until you know the person well enough to be aware how much they can cope with. Find the middle ground between being too soft and coming down like a ton of bricks.
- **Be Specific**. Give examples of the behaviour or work that you are commenting on. If it is behaviour, say honestly what the effects and consequences of this behaviour are.
- **Outcome**. State what changes or improvements you would realistically like to see, and suggest how they could be implemented.
- **Consider feelings**. How might the news you are delivering be received emotionally? The other person needs to be willing to hear what you have to say, and be prepared to act on it. Note their body language, it will give you clues to how they are responding. You may choose to alter your approach if you see they are embarrassed or upset.
- **Structure**. Think about the order in which you deliver your message. Is it logical from the listener's viewpoint? Keep to the subject in hand – do not introduce other issues (*"...and another thing..."*) as this will overwhelm the person.
- **Tone**. You will need to choose an appropriate tone of voice to deliver your message, and back it up with body language that conveys the same meaning. Keep your tone and body language in proportion to the message you are delivering.
- **Clarify understanding**. Never assume that the message given is the message received. Make sure that the other person understands what you are saying, and is not adding meanings that you did not intend.

Modelling

Another behavioural psychologist, Bandura, pointed out that it would take too long to learn everything we need to know by trial and error, by seeing what happens when we do something.

His social learning model (Bandura, 1977) proposes that we also learn "vicariously", that is, by noticing what happens to other people when they do something. We may then copy or model their behaviour, in the hopes of the same rewards (positive reinforcement or absence of negative reinforcement) that we see them receive.

The fact that we base our behaviour on what happens to others provides a powerful tool to use if you want to influence people. You do not have to reward each person in the group before they will put in effort to achieve a certain result. Some go so far as to say that observing what happens to other people is a more powerful motivator (or deterrent) than if it happened to you.

Role models are a powerful learning tool. You as facilitator or leader may well be a role model for your group members. If they perceive you as someone to admire, they may model your approach and interpersonal style. You can use this to set the tone within the session – if you treat every person with care and respect, they are likely to do the same. There is more about this Part Three.

Note, though, that individuals choose their role model based on what is important to them, and where they want to be. You may find other people they can model themselves on – perhaps people closer in age or background, who they can identify with and admire.

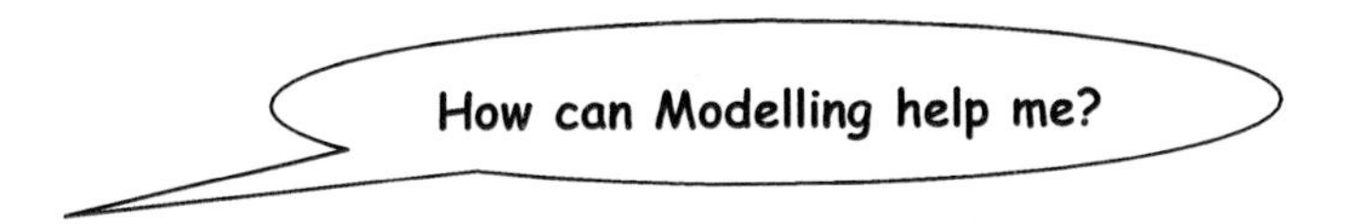

- Try to provide your group with someone to model.

- You can be the model. If so, make sure that your behaviour remains consistently the behaviour you want them to model (it's easy to slip!).
- The model could be one of the learners in the group who they can identify with but who also shows some of the behaviour you want to encourage.
- Showing DVDs of people who are similar to your learners can work well if you feel yourself to be very different from them, whether in age, background, ethnicity, class, etc.

An Example of Successful Modelling

Sofia described her first car accident to her mother and said it was her fault. It didn't sound clear cut, so her mum asked her why she thought she was to blame. She said she assumed so because she was the younger, less experienced driver.

Her mum suggested that she phone the other driver and propose a knock for knock settlement, i.e. both sides pay for their own damage. "I can't do that!" she wailed. "Why not?" "He'll be angry. He had much more damage than me."

They talked about how her big sister would handle the situation - she is more self assured and wouldn't let anyone blame her for an accident that wasn't her fault. Sofia was eventually convinced that she should not assume she was responsible, and to make the phone call.

She did it, and acted as if she was her big sister. Result? The other driver admitted that she was no more at fault than he, and agreed to the settlement. She was delighted!

Preferred Learning Styles

Even if you have never come across any learning theory, you will probably have noticed that what works for some does not work for others. We have already mentioned how different people are drawn to various parts of the learning cycle, which gives us some clues. Honey and Mumford developed their theory of four learning styles (Honey and Mumford, 1992) from Kolb's research. They help people to identify which of the four stages they prefer to operate in. Different individuals tend to have a preference for one of the four stages of the cycle, and Honey and Mumford have named them:

- Activists
- Reflectors
- Theorists
- Pragmatists

This diagram shows how each style relates to the learning cycle:

It is not as simple as falling into one of four boxes: many people prefer a mixture of two, three, or even a fairly equal balance of all four.

On the following pages there is a brief description of each of these four styles. Because people learn in different ways, we need to ensure our session includes learning methods to suit each type.

Honey & Mumford have produced a questionnaire to identify a person's preferred learning style(s). This is currently (Peter Honey, 2010) available to use online. Even without giving people the questionnaire, you can begin to identify each person's preferred learning style and understand why some people lose interest or get frustrated with some activities.

Activists like to involve themselves fully and enthusiastically in new experiences. They enjoy the present and they like to be busy. They learn least well from activities that require them to take a passive role. They can get bored if they do not have things to do.

Activists like:

- ✓ To work in the here and now rather than looking at what happened in the past, or at the wider implications
- ✓ To have a go, even if they get it wrong
- ✓ To do practical tasks
- ✓ Short sessions with plenty of variety
- ✓ To be in the limelight and to lead
- ✓ To have fun

Activists dislike:

- × a passive role (listening, reading, watching)
- × working on their own (writing or homework assignments)
- × repetition (ie: practising over and over again)
- × having to follow detailed instructions precisely
- × to follow a methodical, structured programme with no uncertainties or challenges

So beware of keeping activists waiting too long before you let them loose on an activity. They will get bored sitting and listening, and they may not wait quietly and patiently. If it's essential for them to sit still and listen for a while, some group leaders provide "executive toys" for them to handle while they listen – you can buy these from training suppliers, or just provide coloured pens for them to doodle with. Try to surprise them occasionally!

Your challenge is that people don't grow much from staying in their favourite position on the cycle. You will do your activists a favour if you can encourage them to pause, reflect and draw conclusions, before rushing straight into the next activity. If learning = change, activists will move on more if they try other learning styles as well as their own. But you may need to be firm.

Reflectors like to stand back to ponder experiences and observe them from many different perspectives. They collect data, both first hand and from others, and prefer to chew it over thoroughly before coming to any conclusion. They learn least well from activities that require rapid action with little time for planning.

Reflectors like:

- ✓ To think before they act
- ✓ To prepare thoroughly
- ✓ To watch others and find out how things should be done, before trying for themselves
- ✓ To be given time to think over what has happened
- ✓ Researching, going deeply into things

Reflectors dislike:

- ✗ Being forced into the limelight, eg: role play
- ✗ Having to take action without planning ahead
- ✗ Being expected to obey instructions without fully understanding the reasons
- ✗ Being rushed
- ✗ Not having time to do a thorough job

So beware of assuming a reflector is unintelligent or not interested just because they don't respond or join in quickly. It takes time for them to process what they are hearing, but they are probably taking it in more thoroughly than some other people. You will embarrass them if you spring a question on them without warning, or ask them to perform in front of the group. Their best work may be done in writing in their own time.

Your challenge is to encourage reflectors out of their comfort zone. If they have come to your group to improve their chances at interview, they will possibly resist taking part in role play. But they will not move on unless they do perform – you will be doing them a favour if you force them to move away from reflection into giving it a try. Again, you may need to be firm. But be gentle – they do not like surprises, though if you can get them to move on and take action, they may surprise themselves.

Theorists think problems through in a vertical, step-by-step way, analysing and categorising everything. They gain least from situations that they are unable to research in depth. They value the content of what they are learning more than the process. They will be impatient with too many games and fun activities and with those who enjoy them.

Theorists like:

- ✓ To see the whole picture
- ✓ To be given the theory, concept or model first
- ✓ Ideas presented logically
- ✓ Structure, clear objectives
- ✓ To be intellectually stretched
- ✓ To discuss theories and concepts with other theorists
- ✓ Analytical discussion

Theorists dislike:

- ✗ Unstructured activities, not explained, with no apparent reason for doing them
- ✗ Activities where methods seem unsound or unproven, not planned or structured
- ✗ Not being given clear instructions or guidelines
- ✗ Subjects or fellow learners who appear uninteresting or less intelligent than them
- ✗ Emotions and feelings

So beware of spending so much time keeping your activists amused that you turn off the theorists. You could bring along some in-depth exercises or some thorough background information for them to read if they start to get bored. You might gain their co-operation by explaining your logic: you are catering for a range of needs in this session and everyone can learn from different types.

Your challenge is to move theorists round the learning cycle. If they find emotions difficult, they may lack communication skills. They need to practise these for job interviews and for the world of work, where personal effectiveness is as important as intellectual ability. You could use a theory to persuade them to give it a try – tell them about Kolb's learning cycle!

Pragmatists are practical, down-to-earth people who like making decisions and solving problems. They gain least from sessions where the topic is not related to what they need now. They like to be given tools and techniques they can use to improve things. Once they see the relevance of the subject matter, they want to get on and try it straight away.

Pragmatists like :

- ✓ To see how things will work in practice
- ✓ An early opportunity to try out what they are learning
- ✓ Being taught by someone who is expert in their field
- ✓ To watch demonstrations, be given models and techniques
- ✓ To see the relevance of the topic to their work or their roles

Pragmatists dislike:

- ✗ Learning about something they see no use for
- ✗ Theory that does not appear to take into account the reality of the situation
- ✗ Being asked to do something without a clear explanation or guidelines
- ✗ Too much discussion around the point
- ✗ Grey areas, where there is no one obvious solution

So beware of expecting a pragmatist to enjoy either fun and games or a lot of background theory. They have come to find out how to solve a problem and they will see anything that is not clearly linked to their needs as a waste of time. Invite them to state what they hope to get from the session, and give them a clear structure with an explanation of how you will meet their needs. Use materials and exercises that are up to date and realistic.

Your challenge is to encourage pragmatists to pause, reflect and try a bit of lateral thinking. Life does not always run to a set pattern with ready-made answers, so exploring underlying themes and principles can help them develop better solutions in the longer term. You may need to use practical examples and cases to show them why they need to move around the learning cycle.

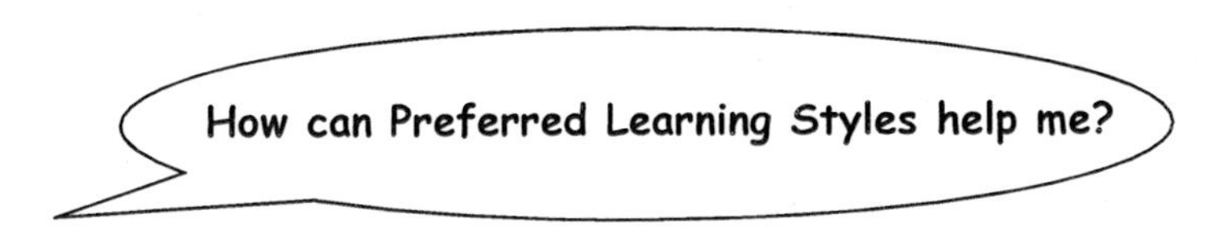

- Knowing how people learn in different ways reminds me to offer a really inclusive learning session.
- As group leaders, we all have our own preferred learning styles. Find out what yours are and remember to move out of your comfort zone to cater for all your learners.

Ann is a Reflector and Theorist: *"I love investigating theories and encouraging the group to discuss around the subject. I can shy away from activities such as role plays and practical case studies."*

Ann needs to step outside her comfort zone to cater for:

- the Activists (or they'll get bored)
- the Pragmatists (or they'll think they're wasting their time)

Julie is an Activist: *"I like to make my sessions lively and fun. I keep people on their toes and they don't have time to get bored."*

Julie may have to slow down to cater for:

- the Reflectors (or they'll feel rushed and left behind)
- the Theorists (who want to go into more depth)

Sensory Based Learning Styles

Neuro-Linguistic Programming (Bandler and Grinder, 1979) suggests each of us has a preferred way of perceiving what goes on around us, a most natural way of taking in information:

Seeing *(NLP term = Visual)*
Hearing *(NLP term = Auditory)*
Touching and Feeling *(NLP term = Kinaesthetic)*

While we all probably learn best through using a combination of all our senses, NLP proposes that there are three types of learner:

- Visual Learners learn most from what they can see
- Auditory Learners learn most from what they can hear
- Kinaesthetic Learners learn most from what they can handle physically or engage with emotionally

"I'm a kinaesthetic learner. I like to engage in practical, hands on experiences. I learn from doing things or being part of them." Julie

"I think I am a visual learner. I'll grasp an idea more easily if I can see it on the page as a diagram, preferably with colour too." Ann

Do remember to vary your methods – only some of your learners will learn most easily from:

- **Listening to** you talking or **Reading** written information
- **Seeing** diagrams and images
- **Doing** something practical or physical

And, don't be offended if people look away when you talk to them or hesitate before answering a question – they might need to translate your input into their own preferred style, before they can understand and respond to it.

Mind Styles – Which Side of the Brain?

Gregorc used studies of the left and right hemispheres of the brain to identify four mind styles, based on how we perceive (take in) and order information (Gregorc, 1982).

Perceiving - Do we prefer information that is...

Concrete?	**or**	**Abstract?**
it comes from our senses, from what we see, hear, etc		it comes from our inner thoughts, from what we imagine, work out

Ordering - Do we like facts and thoughts to be...

Sequential?	**or**	**Random?**
organised, systematic		unstructured, spontaneous

Gregorc's model can be represented as four styles by using his two scales as a matrix:

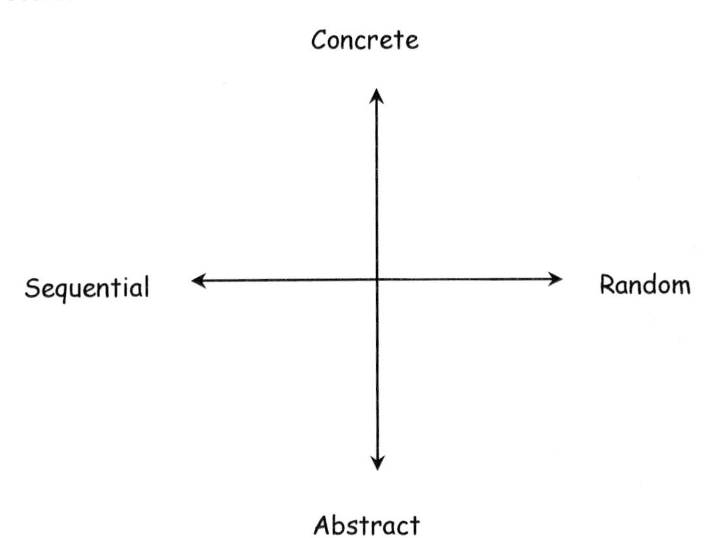

Each quadrant of this matrix provides one of Gregorc's four mind styles. Here is a brief definition of each, suggesting how each type prefers to learn.

Concrete Sequential	**Concrete Random**
They learn from what they can see, hear, touch and feel, in a linear, step-by-step sequence. *You need to provide:* • Instructions • Clear objectives • Short info input • Practical work • Question & Answer	They learn from realistic situations, by using intuition and solving practical problems. *You need to provide*: • Games, simulations • Chance to create products • Choice of options • Experiments • Few restrictions
Abstract Sequential	**Abstract Random**
They are analytical and enjoy a mentally challenging but ordered learning environment. *You need to provide:* • Information and theories • Longer lectures • Working alone • Essays • Research & reading • Discussion/debate	They are emotional and imaginative, and prefer a lively and informal environment. *You need to provide:* • Peer group work, interaction • Discussion • Role play • Using imagination • Short lectures • Humour, music, drama

How can Mind Styles help me?

First – can you work out which type of learner **you** are?

Then – Can you recognise when you automatically use your favourite methods in your group sessions?

Try to offer some learning activities that are outside your comfort zone, to help everyone enjoy their learning.

INFORMATION OVERLOAD

Theorists may have enjoyed this canter through learning theories and be looking forward to the rest of this section.

For everyone else who may be dazed and confused:

Please don't try to remember it all, just gloss over it and keep any nuggets that appeal to you. You might want to look back over it after you have planned a session, and will probably be reassured that you have taken the needs of many types of learner into account already. The more you apply your learning and reflect on it, the sooner it will stick – you might know that already.

Right now, you are the learner! On the next page, you will find an exercise – to apply your learning, as recommended by Gagné.

We have looked at three sets of Learning Styles:

- Honey and Mumford – Four styles
- Sensory Learning – Three styles
- Gregorc's Mind Styles – Four styles

Here is a list of different activities that you could use in your group sessions. What style of learner do you think would enjoy each one? Who might hate each one? *Answers on page 83.*

1. Ask people to get into groups of four and then each person to describe to the others the best job they ever had.
2. Get a new group to stand in a circle and throw a ball to one person at random. Ask them to shout out their name and one fact about themselves, then to throw the ball to another person of their choice who has to do the same, and so on.
3. Give out a sheet with a set of questions which each person has to work on alone and answer by ticking boxes.
4. Divide people into groups of six and ask them to design and deliver (in half an hour's time) to the whole group of 30 a presentation on the topic you are studying – you tell them it can be done however they want – visual, musical, whatever...
5. You give a short presentation (spoken) about what a good CV should look like, then give a set of examples to each person and ask them to produce their own.
6. Give each person modelling dough in four colours and ask them to make something that represents happiness while you tell them about routes into careers in childcare.
7. Show a DVD about interview techniques, then give each person a printed work-sheet with gaps to fill in the correct words.
8. Give each person homework – to research at least five employers in their chosen field and find out specific information about their recruitment methods.

Aptitude – Ability – Intelligence

People have very strong feelings about the concept of intelligence. However, you will probably notice that some people seem to grasp new concepts more quickly than others.

We will explore some of the ways in which psychologists have attempted to differentiate between individuals on the basis of intelligence, to help you think about designing activities to suit every member of your group.

IQ

An early educational psychologist, Binet, wanted to identify children who needed extra support to cope with school work, and he devised a test based on what he thought most children should be able to do at various ages (Binet and Simon, 1916, etc). The test measured each child's "intelligence quotient" (IQ) in relation to the whole population of the same age. The average performance expected at each age was labelled 100, and all children could be placed on a scale with numbers either above or below 100 to show how close their intelligence quotient was to the average for their age. This was devised with the best intentions, to enable the children to catch up with their peers and improve their life chances. Others believed that there was such a thing as "intelligence" that was inherited and they wanted to use testing to identify people in order to differentiate between them, not always for their benefit.

The "nature or nurture" debate (are we shaped more by our genes or by our environment and upbringing?) still rages – not only in relation to intelligence but also to many other physical and psychological features. Many consider that some people can perform certain mental functions (remembering data, sorting data and spotting connections) more quickly and easily than others, and testing is still used in recruitment and selection to appoint people who appear likely to perform best at work or training.

Multiple Intelligences

Most psychologists believe that different people excel in different types of skill – the idea of differential intelligence or multiple intelligences. Guilford proposed 120 different factors making up intelligence (Guilford, 1967). A more manageable number of types of intelligence was proposed by Gardner who suggested that seven different kinds of intelligence act independently of each other in different combinations (Gardner, 1983) – his multiple intelligences:

- Linguistic
- Musical
- Logical – Mathematical
- Spatial
- Bodily Kinaesthetic
- Intrapersonal
- Interpersonal

Some people get confused about the meaning of intrapersonal and interpersonal. Int***ra***personal means how you communicate with yourself, your own internal thoughts and processes that control things like your coping mechanisms, how motivated and disciplined you are. Int***er***personal means how you communicate with others. A good way of remembering this is that the int***er***net allows you to communicate widely with others, whereas an int***ra***net is confined to communication within one organisation.

Many of the psychometric assessment measures used by employers differentiate between people in a similar way, depending on whether they need verbal, numerical, spatial, manual, physical or mechanical skill, or abstract reasoning ability.

Convergent or Divergent Thinking Style

Guilford's work on intelligence also distinguished between two types of thinking – convergent and divergent. We can all do both but many people have a preference for one or the other.

Convergent thinkers prefer to work on problems or questions that have one right answer. They start with a mass of information, and reason through to the solution.

Convergent thinkers perform well at:

- Mathematical calculations
- Crosswords, puzzles and quizzes
- Multiple choice questionnaires

Divergent thinkers prefer to generate a number of different solutions to one question. This ability is more difficult to measure because who is to say how good each solution is?

Some say that conventional examinations and tests favour the convergent thinker, but that the divergent thinker is more likely to solve the most difficult problems, by thinking outside the box, and not needing to rely on what worked in the past.

Prior Learning

It is easier to grasp a new subject if you have already had experience of that type of activity or concept. So-called "intelligence" may have nothing to do with it.

Some people believe that every human is born with an equal capacity to learn every type of skill, but that their environment from the moment they are conceived (or even earlier) will limit the development of some types of skill and favour others.

Can you level the playing field so that everyone can gain from your session, regardless of what they knew before they came? NB: it is quite acceptable for each person to gain something different from your session – catering for this is known as differentiation. Allow for differentiation by setting three levels of objective for your session – What they **must** know, what they **should** know and what they **could** know.

Bite Sized Chunks and Avoiding Indigestion

When we learn something new, it goes first into our short term memory and then may either be forgotten or remembered. For it to be remembered, it has to progress on into the long term memory.

Think of it like eating. We take a mouthful of food and either chew it up and swallow it, or we might spit it out. Once we swallow it, it goes into our digestive system and eventually becomes assimilated into our body. If it's knowledge, it is now in our long term memory and there to be used again when we need it.

Just as the mouth can only hold so much at a time, the short term memory can only hold, we are told, seven pieces of information, and it will only hold them for 15-30 seconds. During that time, if we try to stuff more in, we will have to spit out something, because we cannot exceed seven chunks.

Then we have to do something (chew it up and swallow it) to transfer the seven (or less) items to long term memory, or we will lose them. In our table in Part Three listing Gagné's nine stages of learning we suggest ways to help your group members retain the new information. The theory, coming first from the educationist Piaget, suggests that people can retain information more easily if it fits into a system that they already know (Piaget, 1937, 2002) – for example learning a new language is probably easier if you have already learned a second language. If you are presenting very new concepts, it may take a lot more work for people to retain them.

- Keep new information bite sized - seven new chunks at most.
- Find out how familiar the topic is to them.
- If it is entirely new, give them a longer time with more examples and more repetition, to help them really take it on board.

Learning Curves

The idea that learning progresses in a straight line up from not knowing to knowing, from unskilled to skilled, has been shown to be less straightforward. Various theories relate to this, one showing that it is more of a wavy line with periods when we can't learn however much we try, and then sudden "aha!" moments when it clicks and all falls into place. The way we learn something new is more likely to go like this:

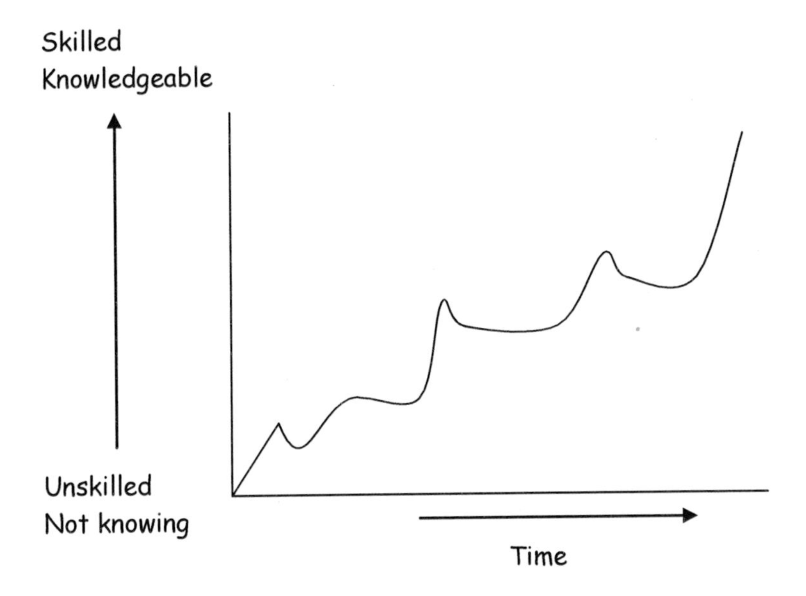

People may even need to unlearn some habits, and the anxiety this can cause is shown by the Consciousness and Competence model (whose origins seem lost in the mists of time):

Level 1 Unconscious Incompetence	**Level 2** Conscious Incompetence	**Level 3** Conscious Competence	**Level 4** Unconscious Competence
You don't know what you don't know….	*You begin to discover that there is a skill to be learnt*	*You begin to use the skill, but it takes concentration and effort*	*You've practised so much that it has become second nature*
☺	☹	😐	☺
I can write a book, it's simple, I'm always writing letters, emails, blogs...	This is awful! Copyright's a minefield; *and* it's too long; *and* it's full of mistakes; *and* people might complain about factual errors, I need to check everything...	Well, I'm getting there, but it's still hard work and I find myself thinking about it day and night....	This is the third book I've written now, I know what needs to be done. I've automatically planned the project. I can do it ***and*** get on with my life.

Julie and Ann spent over a year of trial and error learning to produce the One to One Toolkit. Was it also like this when you learned.... to drive, to touch type, to conduct one to one advice and guidance sessions, to deliver group work?

1. Be prepared for some people to get downhearted if you are showing them new ways to do things.
2. Use this model to encourage yourself and your group. It hurts to feel so incompetent, but with persistence you will get there!

Learning Styles Quiz – The Answers

1. Informal group discussion will probably appeal most to activists and those with abstract random mind styles. Activity allowing for a range of results will suit reflectors and divergent thinkers.
2. An activity requiring movement and physical energy, requiring psychomotor skill, will appeal to kinaesthetic learners. Activists and those with abstract random mind styles will not care if there seems to be no specific objective. Those motivated by social interaction will enjoy the interpersonal aspect.
3. Concrete sequential mind styles and convergent thinkers like questions that have answers. Theorists may enjoy the exercise if it is logical, and pragmatists will if it is realistic and based on a situation linked to their own experience and their objectives for this course.

cont'd....

....cont'd

4. This kind of open ended project will appeal most to the abstract random mind style. Activists and those with a concrete random mind style will enjoy it if other group members provide the framework and keep them on task. Pragmatists will enjoy it if they can use the end product in their own work situation. Visual learners may enjoy producing the visuals, and kinaesthetic learners will enjoy the hands on approach.

5. Pragmatists will like the clear instructions and practical task relevant to their needs. Theorists may like the presentation, if it's giving them new information and is presented logically and makes sense.

6. Activists will enjoy having something to do. Kinaesthetic learners and those with a concrete random mind style will work best with a practical, hands-on task.

7. Completing the worksheet will probably appeal most to convergent thinkers and those with a concrete sequential mind style. Pragmatists will appreciate the DVD if it appears realistic.

8. Reflectors and those with the abstract sequential mind style will like researching and exploring without limitations, though reflectors may have difficulty summarising their findings in a logical, compact format.

Do you agree with us?

Have we left out any type of learner?

Why ?

Why Do People Want To Learn?

Everything we've discussed up to here will fall on deaf ears if your group are not motivated. Developing skills and knowledge is hard work and it requires energy, both mental and physical. Motivation provides that energy.

Walk into a room of people and you can gauge their motivation and energy levels at a glance. Are they:

- bright eyed, smiling, leaning forward in anticipation?
- lying back in their seats, yawning, eyeing you with suspicion?
- deep in their own conversations, backs to you?

Most adults have learned a veneer of politeness, so their lack of motivation might be less obvious than in a class of 14 year olds, but they have their own ways of showing enthusiasm, and lack of it. So how can you tap into their potential energy sources and fire them up so that they will learn?

Maslow's Hierarchy of Needs

You may have come across Maslow's hierarchy (Maslow, 1987) in one-to-one advice and guidance work. He suggests that everyone is motivated by their needs and that these can be categorised into five types. He also says that some needs are more basic and essential than others, and until we feel sure that our more basic needs are met, we will not be motivated by the "higher" order ones. You will often find the five categories of needs presented as a pyramid. Maslow and other humanist psychologists believed that we are all aiming for Self Actualisation, which means to become what we truly are or have the potential to be. However, we will not be free to care about achieving self-actualisation until our lower order needs have been met.

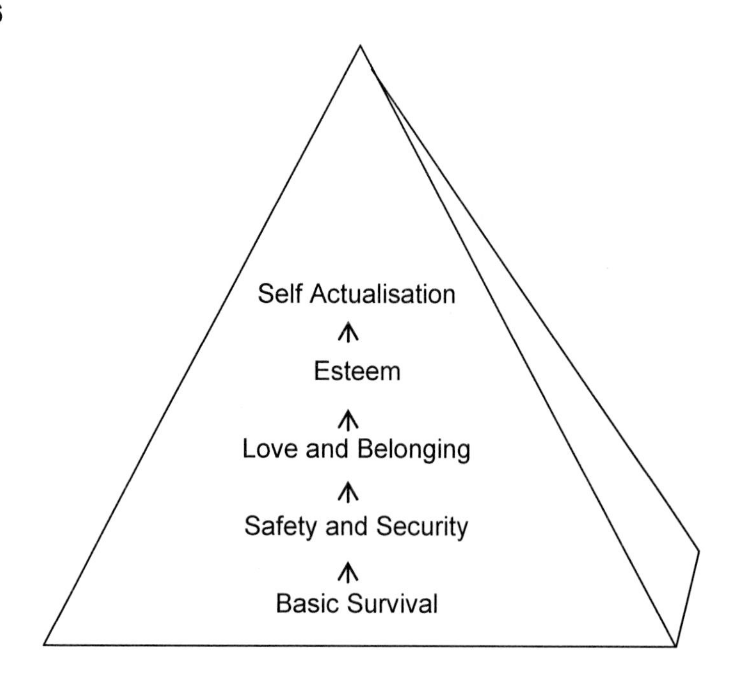

What does this mean for your groupwork session? Two people are attending your session on how to write a CV. What is their motivation? One tells you she has been bringing up a family for the last fifteen years and wants to get a job because she feels under-valued now her children are out all day at secondary school. Perhaps her motivation is driven by her need for Esteem (which includes Self-Esteem).

The other is 18 years old and left school with no qualifications. He's quite happy on the dole and hanging out with his mates. His motivation for attending the session is the threat of withdrawal of his benefits - a need for Basic Survival. Mrs Self Esteem and young Mr Basic Survival are unlikely to respond in the same way to your carefully planned set of activities, nor to your personal style. In your advance planning, trying to put yourself into their shoes will help you understand where they are coming from and how to motivate them.

Levels of Motivation for Learning

Motivation can either be extrinsic or intrinsic. In the context of groupwork, extrinsic means that our drive to learn comes from sources outside of us, i.e. external sources. An example would be if we are threatened with punishment if don't attend, or our parents have promised a reward if we do.

Intrinsic means that the drive comes from within ourselves. We might want to learn, or change, for many different reasons.

Another theoretical model develops this by suggesting your group members may have any one of four types of motivation for attending your session:

Instrumental - Social - Achievement - Expressive

Extrinsic ←——————→ *Intrinsic*

- Instrumental - *Need to gain reward or avoid harm*
- Social - *Desire to be socially accepted*
- Achievement - *Need to succeed, do well*
- Expressive - *Interest in the subject, love of learning*

As you can see, if we have an expectation that our clients are coming to a groupwork session purely because they want to gain new skills, we could be sadly deluded; other factors could be well be at work.

It is also worth bearing in mind that motivation can be fluid. A young person or a woman returner may initially attend a group session because of external pressure, but if they gain benefit from the session, their motivation may change - they could return for another session because their enthusiasm has grown now that they can see the group activities will bring a positive change to their lifestyle or employment prospects. Alternatively they may just start to enjoy being part of the group, gaining satisfaction from being socially accepted. You can take steps to increase their motivation by, for example, making sure they make friends and have fun while they are there.

You can see themes from Maslow's hierarchy here, but please don't see each level as completely independent of the others. Reality is often more complex than theory, with several motivators operating at any one time, some of which may be within your control while others are just a lucky chance. Take the example of an Interview Skills Workshop - if I'm attending to keep a nagging spouse at bay when I really have little interest in working, my motivation will be extrinsic, and probably slight. If, however, I book the session and then a good friend tells me about an excellent part time vacancy available now in a field I'd enjoy, suddenly my motivation becomes focused and stronger.

The Difference between Children and Adults

Motivation is a key area where you will find a difference between working with children and adults. As we mature, we become more likely to be motivated to gain skills because we have a practical application for the learning, such as to cook meals we like, drive our own car, or use the computer to store our photos. Malcolm Knowles is a theorist who has looked at the differences between educating children and adults, recognising that adults bring very different things to the groupwork session (Knowles, 1984). Educational theory has long been known as **pedagogy** – based on Greek words for "children learning". Knowles calls his theory of how adults learn **andragogy** (using more Greek). He suggests that:

- As an individual matures, his self-concept moves from one of being a dependent personality towards being a self-directed person.
- An adult has a growing reservoir of experience to draw on and learn from.

- Her readiness to gain skills and knowledge becomes increasingly oriented towards the roles she plays in life and how they develop.
- He becomes problem centred, not subject centred, and expects to quickly find a use for the knowledge gained.

I work with adults - how can andragogy help me?

- Make sure you utilise the group's experience
- Remember that your aim is to help group members move towards being self directed - if they are becoming increasingly dependent on you, you have a problem. If there is time, why not invite adult learners to participate actively in the planning?
- Make explicit the link between the content and their real life challenges and concerns, so that they see how the session can help them deal with these.

I work with 14-19's - how can andragogy help me?

- Most of your group members won't come with objectives they want to achieve, so you'll need to find another way to motivate them. If they enjoy the process, the here and now of the session, you'll be half way there. Offer them some fun.
- Put more effort into engaging with them as a person rather than expecting the subject matter to thrill them.
- Some subject matter will interest them – find out what, and use it. With young adults, topics like personality, relationships and role models could be your way in.

- Many are motivated by achievement, so offer them the chance to compete and win – quizzes, team games, or problems to solve.

- They may be more accustomed to taking a passive role and being told what to do by adults, rather than taking responsibility for their own development. Give them clear instructions if you want them to work independently, and keep your eyes open to prevent them wandering off track.

- Most adolescents are very concerned with social acceptance and feeling they belong with their peers. They may achieve more social recognition by rebelling than by co-operating. You need to assert your presence and work harder to keep them focused on the task. Use your sense of humour to deal with their distractions without getting upset – try to make a joke of it.

- They may have a lot more physical energy than adults, with a shorter attention span. Their bite size chunks need to be short and varied. However, as with adults, just because they are younger does not mean they are all the same. They will have the full range of learning styles – young theorists will not want to be treated like activists and given all fun and games with no underpinning theory.

- Finally, your group members are in the process of moving from childhood to adulthood, and will want to be treated as adults. Your challenge is to know when to use methods best suited to pedagogy and when to adopt those that work best with adults.

Process and Content

When we looked at the affective domain, we saw how you need to manage the process of your group session as well the content. An enjoyable process could be the key for people whose motivation to attend your session is instrumental or social. Part Four has more to say about group dynamics and how to manage them – once people feel happy in the group, they are free to learn what you plan to teach them.

A Final Word about Ethics and Client centred Groupwork

Most of the things you can do to motivate all your learners are those that make them feel good about themselves. This fits well with the major ethical principles that underpin advice and guidance work:

- respect, equality and impartiality
- empowerment and autonomy
- beneficence (ensuring clients' well-being)

You can apply these principles to:

- The venue you choose
- The way you arrange the seating
- Catering for any special needs
- How you greet people on arrival
- Ground rules you agree about working together
- How you respond and provide feedback to individuals
- The activities you design
- How you share your attention between individuals
- How you deal with the unexpected, or with "difficult" people

Bear in mind especially individuals who may feel different from the rest of the group. They may feel different because of their age, gender, religion, culture, style of dress, wealth, accent, lifestyle, disability, learning style, language. They will feel even more uncomfortable if you seem to be like the rest of the group. You need to put special effort into welcoming them and ensuring you use language, examples and activities that they can relate to.

How can ethics help me?

Part Three takes you into the practical and active world of DOING. In the heat of the moment, your ethical framework will help you remain professional and client centred.

Part Three
Planning the Session

Enough of the theory! In this section we roll up our shirtsleeves and get very practical, giving you the tools of the trade to prepare and run a successful group session. You will find out how to prepare and structure your session, with lots of ideas for exercises, different ways of getting your message across and some example session plans that you can use or adapt to save you time.

If you come across anything here that doesn't quite add up and you've skipped reading the theory in Part Two, it may be worth going back and leafing through, to see the thinking behind the activities. Use the index to find a particular topic. On the other hand, if you've read the theory and you're wondering how on earth to apply it and turn it into action, you should find some answers here.

We've already seen why a group session needs to be more adviser-led than a one to one advice session. Even in client-led one to one work, a model structure can help the adviser keep it focused and effective. For your group session, you will definitely need a session plan.

So what needs to be planned?

- the **content** – the tasks to be achieved
- the **process** – how we go about the tasks

We have combined a few of the models from Part Two to provide a structure for your session. This structure is geared towards one stand-alone session rather than part of a series. It is not prescriptive, but it does give you a good starting point. You can adapt it if your particular group has an agenda that does not include all six stages.

Later, we'll look at how to produce your session plan. For now, we are going to concentrate on considering how we can achieve each stage of the model. If you take an idea or two from each section, you will already have the bare bones of a session plan.

Here is the model:

1	Focus their Attention *and* Break the Ice
2	Agree Learning Objectives *and* Set Ground Rules
3	Recall Prior Learning *and* Present New Learning
4	Allow Performance *and* Provide Feedback
5	Evaluate Learning *and* Prepare for Ending
6	Plan Next Steps *and* Say Good Bye

And for those of you in a hurry, on the next three pages is a quick overview of some of the suggestions we give in the rest of Part Three, where we discuss each stage in a lot more detail.

Stage	Suggestions
1 How will I get their attention? And keep it! *More detail on page 98*	Find out before the session: • What's their history and background? • What else is likely to be on their minds? • What do they care about? Choose something from your findings and link it into your opening remarks. Start with High Energy! Make an impact! Surprise them. Ask questions. Be observant throughout: Note what is competing for their attention and deal with it, by: • Discussing it. • Using it as an example of a learning point. • Giving him/her something to do.
2 How will I agree the objectives with them? *More detail on page 110*	Ask them what they want to get from the session. Link what they tell you to the objectives you had already planned for the session. Reassure them that they will get what they want, tailoring your planned input to what they tell you.
3a. How will I help them recall what they know already? *More detail on page 122*	If possible, find out beforehand what they know already. At the start, ask them what they already know – they may actually learn from each other. Prepare questions, a quiz or discussion to find out. Link your new information to their existing knowledge. Refer back to what they have told you.

Stage	Suggestions
3 b. How will I present the new learning to them? *More detail on page 125*	Vary your methods - Take them through each stage of Kolb's Learning Cycle: Present information, allow activity, encourage reflection and let them draw their own conclusions and plan action. Divide information into chunks and present it in an organised manner. Use a variety of media – spoken, written, visual, diagrams. Use methods to suit all learning styles. Help them link it to what they already know. Provide different examples. Describe it in different ways. Tell stories to illustrate it. Make it relevant to their lives or job roles. Rhymes, Mnemonics, Repetition, Problems to solve.
4 a. How will I enable them to perform? *More detail on page 135*	Provide opportunities for them to apply learning to different problems in a variety of situations. Give them things to do: Practice, Things to make, Tests or Questions to answer, Present to each other, Games, Case studies to discuss. Simulations. Exercises. Tasks. Assignments. Role play. Present to the group. Written answers to questions. Real life trials.
4 b. How will I feed back on their progress? *More detail on page 142*	Short comments throughout the session. Provide information on performance, in comparison with a standard. Remember the rules of feedback and the effects of positive reinforcement.

Stage	Suggestions
5 How will I evaluate their progress? *More detail on page 147*	Unless you are training people for a qualification, you may not need to do a final assessment. Ask them to evaluate what they have gained from your session. Give them a form to complete – one they can keep, incorporating an action plan. Asking them to complete an evaluation or feedback form for **you** is a separate exercise.
6a. What next steps should I plan with them? *More detail on page 154*	Ask them how they can reinforce this new learning and put it into practice? Ask them what further help they need and how they can get it. Add your own suggestions. Give handouts and further exercises. Suggest further practice tasks.
6b. How should we say Good-Bye? *More detail on page 157*	Summarise what they have achieved during the session. Encourage them to value the steps forward, and be proud of their own efforts. Praise and celebrate.

1 Focus Attention *and* Break the Ice

First Things First

When does your group session actually begin? Some people will turn up early, others may drift in after the advertised start time. At a given point, you must decide to make a start. The need to focus people's attention is one difference between individual and group work. At the same time you still have to consider individuals' anxieties and fears, and remember to create an appropriate atmosphere right from the very first contact - which can be difficult, because *your* attention may well be on other things (the projector, the layout, finding enough pens...). Remember that they will interpret every facial expression as an indication of your attitude towards them. We have already covered many of the basics of setting a group at ease in Part One, when we discussed creating a friendly, encouraging atmosphere.

You need to engage and motivate your group and to allow it to form. You want members to get to know each other and to feel:

- I like being here
- I feel comfortable
- It's going to be fun / interesting
- It will be useful to me
- I want to join in and give it my best
- I will stop thinking about my to-do list, stop talking to my friends, and give this my full attention

Stop and think about your group – which of the above will need more work? A group who already work or play together, gathered in their own school or workplace, may need less of the ice-breaking and more of the focus. The reverse is probably the case with a group who have come together for the first time on premises they don't know.

First, we'll look at how you grab the group's attention and focus it on the activities you've planned. Then we'll provide a Toolkit of ice breakers that have worked well for us.

Focusing their Attention

There may be distractions – it may seem more fun to carry on talking about what happened at the pub last Saturday, to flirt with the boys in the group, to catch up on the gossip from friends or colleagues you haven't seen for a while.

Then there may be anxieties – you have a feud with another person in the group, all the other people look cleverer than you, you don't want to speak out in front of everyone. Sitting still and listening might be the most boring thing to you. You don't like the look of the group leader standing up there at the front, he reminds you of someone you used to know.

The best way of making sure you get everyone's attention is to be democratic and share yourself around equally between all the learners, so that no one falls through the net. This includes smiles and eye contact as you present to the whole group and the amount of time you allow each person to speak – balanced with the fact that some prefer to remain in the background.

Toolkit for Focusing Attention

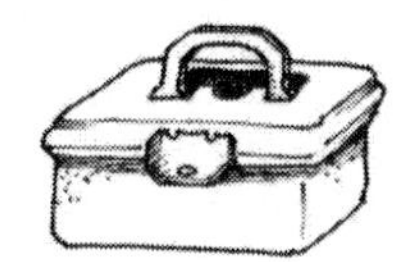

1. Use your Body

You need to be noticed! Your body language needs to counter their reasons for not wanting to focus. Body language speaks volumes and will override any words you speak, so give it sufficient attention. If you are not sure what your body language conveys, ask a colleague for some honest feedback or watch yourself on video.

The message is:

Hey, notice me, I am here, Now!
I am a nice person, I like you and you'll like me.
I know I can make this interesting and useful to you.
I'm confident and well organised.
This is going to be fun too, you will enjoy it.

How are you going to convey this message? A short cut is to believe it yourself – our body language always showcases our feelings, so you must feel and believe your own message. We discuss this further in Part Four – Rule No 1. Meanwhile, here are some hints:

- Take a deep breath
- Stand up straight – shoulders back, head up, chest out
- Eye contact with group members – a firm gaze, shared between all, moving round the room as you speak
- Smile as you would if welcoming friends to your home
- Slow, calm movements – nothing too jerky
- Open posture – arms out away from your body, open hands
- Take another deep breath
- Inject plenty of energy
- Voice – loud enough – aim it at the people at the back of the room
- Slow, calm voice – you want everyone to hear and understand
- Plenty of pauses – pause after each phrase of a few words – look at people especially during your pauses as if to say "this is important – I know you want to really take it in"

"Hi / Good morning"

(pause, breathe, smile, eye contact)

"My name's Ann / Ann Reynolds"

(pause, breathe, smile, eye contact)

"I work for CareerTrain and I'm a Guidance Adviser"

(pause, breathe, smile, eye contact)

"It's good to see you all here...."

(pause, breathe, smile, eye contact)

2. **Ask a question**

If your group appears interested and focused already, you could simply introduce yourself.

If not, or as a follow on, a question is a useful tool for drawing people in. As guidance advisers, you already know that the best questions are open questions:

- Why are we here?
- Who am I?
- How are you today?

If you ask a question, you will have decided what kind of answers you are expecting and what you'll do with the answers; and what you'll do if no one replies.

Why are we here? can lead neatly into your next task – agreeing objectives – you can confirm or correct their perceptions – if you have a flip chart, you can write down everyone's ideas and then go through and explain which you will cover and how. You will acknowledge every idea (however off the wall it may be), to build everyone's confidence at this early stage.

Who am I? can help you introduce a bit of humour as you field the responses – depending on how well they know you. It allows you to introduce yourself but raises their energy levels – having to think how to answer the question, plus taking a breath of air to speak, both get the heart beating a bit faster and wake people up, whereas just listening is passive and more likely to send them off to sleep.

How are you today? is a question we often use when meeting people who are likely to be unhappy or angry. If we are worried the session might get off to a negative start, we give out an A4 sheet of cartoon faces showing lots of different moods and we ask people to work in pairs and choose one or two faces that most closely express what they feel. Feeding back can be more orderly than a free for all – as each pair says their piece, we acknowledge what they say (write words on flip chart?) – empathise and say how we hope our session will help. We can be honest and realistic by admitting there will be limits to what we can do about it, while still showing that we care. Allowing feelings to be expressed early on can defuse a possible explosion later at the storming stage (see group dynamics in Part Four). This question "*How are you today?*" can also help people express their shyness or fears about the session, and lead us into explaining how we work (respect, kindness, etc).

What's on your mind? We know that we are competing for people's attention with other, often more pressing, concerns. We want them to put these to one side for the duration of our session, so that they can focus on what we have to offer them. One colleague has an excellent way of getting people to articulate their concerns and then put them to one side. She gives each a small piece of paper and asks them to write down the distracting concern (or they could draw it if they don't like writing). She then walks round with a bin and asks them to screw up the paper and throw it in. Symbolic physical gestures like this can work wonders, not least by releasing pent up feelings in a fun way. People don't need to tell anyone what they wrote on the paper, but to quote our colleague: "it's a good way of forgetting about cross husbands, late trains, unpaid bills and a whole range of other things".

Rhetorical questions – ones you answer yourself – are an absolute no-no in one to one advice and guidance. However, they can have a place at this Focusing stage of a group session. They serve the purpose of waking people up, while allowing you to rescue them by providing the answer, once you have aroused their interest.

- How long does the average employer spend reading each CV that crosses her desk?
- What's the worst thing that can happen at an interview?
- Is there such a thing as the perfect job?
- How many people look forward to job interviews?
- Is money more important than job satisfaction?
- How many 16 year olds from this school got apprenticeships last year?

It doesn't really matter if the question is impossible to answer. In fact only the last one of these could be answered with any degree of accuracy, though you might find research that provides an answer to the CV question (we've heard it's half a minute).

Nor does it matter whether people come in with answers to the question – if they do, of course you will acknowledge their input, and then go on to what you wanted to say. The point of asking questions is to make your job easier – the job of focusing attention.

3. Surprise them

There was a time when job vacancies came to careers offices on continuous print-outs that were usually torn at the folds into separate job cards. One adviser used to introduce herself to classes of year 11 students by taking in a long stream of these still joined up vacancy cards. It was a period of high unemployment and she wanted to show these school leavers that there were still jobs out there.

She would first ask a question like "How many jobs for school leavers do you think we've got at the careers centre?". Then she'd let the cards unfold and as they reached the floor, she'd lift her flowing skirt and climb in her Doc Martens first onto the chair, and then onto the teacher's desk as the cards opened out like a concertina down to the floor. She generally got their attention as she made her point, and could go on to deliver her message through activities using the vacancy cards.

This was a surprise for the group because teachers didn't generally do that kind of thing. It worked because it was relevant and carried a message linked to the topic of the session. Depending on how much of a performer you are, you can choose all manner of ways to surprise your audience. Here are some ideas:

- A joke
- An item of costume
- Something bright and colourful that moves or makes a noise
- A piece of music
- A work of art – poster, picture, small statue, ornament

- An artefact from previous times
- A new gizmo or gadget

In fact, anything as long as it has some relevance to the topic and does not patronise your audience by being too childish. If you are seeking inspiration, try thinking through your five senses. Julie still remembers her very first French lesson: “The teacher began by giving us Camembert. I’d never tasted it before so it has stuck in my mind ever since.”

You may also be aware of the danger of over-stimulating certain audiences – if they are already lively, your surprise might tip them over into a riot. You may need to make a judgement call about whether to use the planned surprise when you assess the atmosphere in the room.

Toolkit - Ice Breakers

1. Questions to discuss in pairs

After a very short introduction by you, ask the group to work in pairs, usually with the person they happen to be sitting next to. Give them one or more (up to three) questions to answer, each in turn, ready to feed back to you and the whole group. Questions should be easy to answer, and you can try to make them fun too. They will depend on who is in the group and what you know about their background, also how well they already know each other. We have used:

- Tell us three things most people don’t already know about you.
- Describe your day so far.
- Tell us about one item of clothing you are wearing – or the last item you bought.
- Take one thing from your pocket or bag and tell us what it says about you.

- Take relevant initials (eg: for a CV session, the letters C and V) and talk about one C and one V that is important to you. Of course, you can use their own initials too.
- Tell us about this school / your workplace / where you live / this area: the best thing, the worst thing and one interesting thing.

If you use this exercise, it's important first to establish the ground rules about Confidentiality (will anything go outside this room?) and the Right to Remain Silent (you can choose what information you do and do not share about yourself).

If you want to get them moving around, there are many ways of dividing them into pairs or small groups besides working with the person next to them. Here are some ideas:

- Find the person whose birthday is nearest yours
- Get every other person to move round one
- Find someone wearing a similar colour/hairstyle, pair of shoes to you
- Count round, going up to half of the group number, then start again. They have to work with the person who has the same number as them.
- Work with the person sitting opposite
- Choose someone you don't know very well

As you can see, many of these ideas are icebreakers in themselves. They are also useful for energising groups later in the session - it can keep them alert if they are never quite sure how they are going to be divided!

2. Play ball

Have a soft ball, bean bag or similar. You ask a simple question such as:

- Is anyone's birthday in January?
- Who's got a cat?
- Has anyone here got a black car?

The first person who says "me" is the one you throw the ball to. They then say their name and throw the ball to anyone they choose. That person catches the ball, says their name and throws it to someone they choose. Carry on till everyone has caught the ball and said their name. People really do need to be sitting or standing in a circle for this to work – but we believe sitting in a circle, square or horseshoe is more friendly anyway, certainly better than sitting in rows.

3. Repeating names

Go round the room asking each person to say their name. They should put an adjective in front of their name that starts with the same letter, for example "I'm Anxious Ann" or "I'm Joyful Julie". The next person has to repeat the previous person's name and then state their own: "That's Anxious Ann and I'm Joyful Julie". The next person has to start repeating the first person's name, then the second, then their own.

As you go round the circle there are more names to remember, which makes it harder, but the names get repeated, which helps. Other group members can come in and help out if the person gets really stuck. Instead of getting each person to give themselves an adjective, you could ask them to say "My name is .... And my favourite animal is a ...." Or "my favourite colour is ..." Choose whatever feels right for this group.

4. Who are you?

Asking people to introduce themselves and give a bit of information about their background is the most obvious activity at this forming stage (see Group Dynamics in Part Four) of your group. Depending on the type of course you are running, you and the other group members might like to know: What is their job role? What organisation do they work for? What previous experience have they got of job interviews? How did they find out about today's session? One adviser facilitating a session about careers in child care asked every person to say what their favourite toy was when they were young.

5. Arrange yourselves into alphabetical order

An idea suggested by Jenny Rogers in her book "Adults Learning" (Rogers, 2007) is especially good for making sure no one gets excluded if some, but not all, of the members already know each other. Re-arranging themselves means that everyone has to speak to everyone else and get to know their names. People are energised by the action of getting up from their seats and talking – you can help them focus this energy to use in your session. If they all know each other really well, you could use some other order, eg:

- Distance travelled to get here today
- Birthdays, starting with January
- Height
- Place of birth on a north to south range

6. Word Association

Make a pack of cards with a word or phrase on each one. Lay them out and ask everyone to choose three cards, then explain to the group or a partner why they chose those particular cards. Here are some ideas for what to put on the cards:

- Personal attributes (Words like: kind, friendly, calm, smiley, serious, thoughtful, lively, talkative, independent, etc)

- Skills (Phrases or words like: being on time, organised, maths, writing, filling in forms, gardening, using the internet, speaking up for myself, following instructions, having ideas, being creative, decorating, etc)
- Job Titles

7. Bingo

Give everyone a handout you have prepared earlier with a table something like this on it:

Likes football	Can draw	Has a dog
Has a brother and a sister	Went to the cinema in the last month	Likes gardening
Watches the Simpsons	Goes to the gym	Uses the library

You can make up the contents depending on the group. Ask them to circulate and talk to each other to find someone who fits in each box. As the purpose is to break the ice, it does not matter if your group fails to yield someone for every box. By briefly discussing the results you can soon build up a picture of the group members.

8. Home Improvement

Give each pair a small household or office item (or even a toy) and ask them what they would do to improve it. This might be difficult for them to get into, so give them an example to give them the idea, eg:

"Here's my tea strainer. It's a bit small for my favourite mug, so I'd make it a bit bigger, with a better hook on it. It's getting a bit discoloured so I'd like it to be stain proof, in red to match the mug."

Of course, ideas like this are fun but not directly related to the content of the session. You could adapt this idea and use objects that are related to the session, for example:

- Leaflets from different agencies – Ask them:
    - *How could you make this leaflet better?*
    - *Is it clear what the agency does?*
    - *Do you like the colour and print size? Graphics?*
- Job adverts – Ask them:
    - *What's good about this job ad? What's bad?*
    - *Does it tell you what you need to know? Anything missing?*
    - *What would make it perfect?*
- Pictures of people – Say:
    - *These people are dressed for an interview at a shop/office/factory.*
    - *What would you change about them to make them better dressed?*
    - *What do you like about what they are wearing?*

This last set of activities has enough content to be part of your learning session – stages 3 or 4 of your plan – "present new learning" or "allow performance" to see how much they have learned. You can use the same activity for different purposes.

2 Agree Objectives *and* Ground Rules

When we looked at transferring your skills in Part One, we saw that agreeing learning objectives and ground rules is very similar to contracting in one to one work. Here is an overview of the things you may need to agree with your group, adapted from The One to One Toolkit. You won't need to cover every point at every session – just use it as a checklist and pick the points you need in your particular circumstances to make it applicable to groupwork.

Contracting Checklist

Process	Content/Scope	Ethical Boundaries
Timing How long will the session be? Is there a break? When? How long? **Health and Safety** Where is the fire exit and the muster point? Is the alarm tested today? **Administration** If you are completing learner records or other paperwork, you need to explain how and why. **Structure** An indication of the types of activity you will be undertaking together, and in what order.	**Roles & Responsibilities** Who you are Who you work for Your expertise and/or experience **Topic/Subject** Breadth Depth, or level **Aims** What is the general goal of the session? **Objectives** aka **Learning Objectives** or **Intended Learning Outcomes** What will you have achieved by the end of the session?	**Ground rules** The behaviour you expect for the group to work together successfully Confidentiality boundaries

Ground Rules

Using a set of ground rules is one way of establishing boundaries, and reinforcing the aims of the session. This may sound overly formal, and may not be necessary with all groups, but it is no bad thing to draw up a list. If you suspect that participants may be unruly, or if working in a group is unfamiliar territory for them and they may not know the behaviour that is expected, ground rules can be very helpful. Setting ground rules can also allay fear to some degree, as people will have a better idea of what to expect.

What is even more important is that you have thought through in advance the issues outlined below, so that you are clear in your own mind how you want your session to proceed.

Ground rules should be about topics such as comfort, safety, and productivity. If you have plenty of time, you can discuss with the group in order to agree ground rules, but when time is tight, a practical alternative is to present them with a set, and ask if they can agree to them, or if they want any changes or additions.

Be sure to keep your ground rules as brief and understandable as possible - we are trying to gain commitment, not incite rebellion! Here is an example we have used successfully with different groups:

Ground Rules

- Treat others with respect
- Be prepared to share your knowledge and experience so that others can benefit
- Respect confidentiality
- Say if you don't understand
- Tell us if you are not happy with anything
- Be punctual
- Keep your phone off
- Enjoy it!

Of course, there are many more ground rules you might set. Below is an eclectic list of other examples we have seen; mostly just variations on the themes above. The ones you choose will depend on the nature of the group, the purpose of the session, and your style as group leader.

Take a note of the rules you would find helpful to use in your own practice, then you will have a starting point that you can fine tune to meet your own needs when the time comes - but remember not to overload your group with rules and regulations. They are supposed to help, not hinder!

More Potential Ground Rules.........

- Arrive and start on time
- Keep to the topic
- Speak one at a time
- Listen to different ideas without putdowns
- Support each other
- Be open and honest
- Respect others
- Withhold judgment and negative comments
- Participate, don't dominate
- Don't interrupt
- Each person is responsible for their own behaviour
- Listen to others
- Speak up for yourself
- Respect the room and the equipment
- Be open to hearing other points of view
- No swearing

Objectives

In one to one work, you have an overall aim of moving your client forward, but the actual objectives will emerge as you contract with the client. When you offer a groupwork session, you have to decide the aims and set the objectives in advance, at the planning stage. They will usually be more specific and targeted – partly because you can't follow each individual's wishes as they emerge. People come to a CV workshop for a reason – they expect it to be about CV's.

It is an essential part of good practice to state your aims and objectives at the start of your session plan. You will then present them to the group at the beginning of the session, and maybe modify them in discussion, if you feel it is appropriate.

So what's the difference between an aim and an objective?

Aims

Your aim is usually a general concept. It expresses an ideal, and gives an overview of what you want to achieve. The aim is what people really want and what draws them in. It often has an emotional appeal. For example:

- To make participants more competitive in the job market.
- To improve people's management skills.
- To help people perform better at interviews.
- To raise people's career aspirations.
- To make people aware that I am here to help them.
- To encourage more people to use the advice service.

Objectives – Intended Learning Outcomes

Objectives are steps towards achieving the aim. They are more specific and measurable than aims. It may take years for you to know whether the aims have been achieved, but you and the group members should be able to see whether objectives have been met by a specific time (often "by the end of this session"). The educational world now uses the term "Intended Learning Outcomes", defined thus:

What the learners will know and be able to do as a result of engaging in the learning process

How will you express your objectives? You can use SMART to help you. Remember that SMART is an acronym for:

- Specific - S can also be Stretching, when applied to learning
- Measurable
- Achievable - or Attractive or Appealing (depending on context)
- Realistic - or Relevant
- Time bound

Some say that learning outcomes should also be behavioural and observable – people should do something different to show that they have learned. Not everyone agrees with this, but the idea can help you keep your objectives realistic and focused.

In Part Two we looked at the three domains of learning – Cognitive, Psychomotor and Affective – often expressed more plainly as Knowledge, Skills and Attitudes. So your objectives can start:

- By the end of this session, participants will know....
- By the end of this course, students will be able to....
- By the end of this session, group members will feel....

You may be wondering how objectives that say *"group members will feel...."* can be specific and measurable. One way to measure objectives about feelings is to ask them at the beginning of the session, or before it, something like *"On a scale of 1-10, how confident do you feel about applying for jobs?".* By asking the same question afterwards, you have a measure of their affective learning (ie: how their feelings have changed). Of course it is a subjective measure, but feelings are subjective. Before and after questionnaires can be a good tool both to get measures for your evaluation, and also to help your learners see their progress. As a general rule of thumb – if you didn't measure it at the start, don't expect to be able to measure the progress at the end!

You can see some examples of aims and objectives we have set in our session plans, at the end of this Part Three.

Remember that once you have stated your objectives or intended learning outcomes, you will have a clear benchmark for your end of session evaluation. This awareness may influence the objectives that you set – the more specific they are, the easier it is to tell whether you have met them!

Toolkit for Agreeing Objectives and Ground Rules

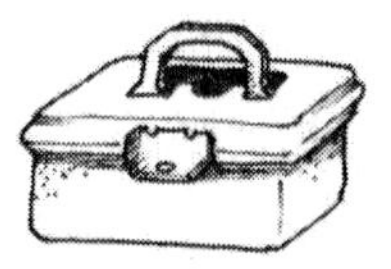

Now you know what aims and objectives should look like, and have decided what they are, how will you agree them with your group? You may use:

- Presentation
- Discussion

Presentation

Presentations can be visual and/or spoken. For example:

1. A short spoken introduction by you to the whole group

When you welcome people and focus their attention, at the same time you can say a few words about the purpose of the session and what the programme is. You may well combine your spoken presentation with one or more of the visual presentation methods.

2. Poster, Leaflet or Web page

People might see your first presentation before they arrive at the group session. You can prepare a leaflet, a web page, or a poster. This can be a useful visual aid to reinforce your message – "What you can expect from the session" and "What we will cover". It might be what attracted them to the course. Ann and a colleague used this:

Job Hunting? You can do it!

Come and find out
how to..

Do Better in

JOB INTERVIEWS

Thursday 15th July

☺ small group (no more than 12)
☺ very friendly, informal atmosphere
☺ time to chat and share experiences
☺ see a DVD of an interview
☺ get some practice
☺ have booklets to keep

3. PowerPoint

Use a PowerPoint slide to focus attention. You can prepare professional looking slides in advance and also print paper copies to give out to individuals. Again, it's a visual means of communication.

Then you can ask the group if they agree with the objectives and ground rules, or if they want to add any others or negotiate. How you handle this depends on the make-up of the group. Be prepared to go with the majority – but, if some rules are set in stone, then stand firm and say so.

You can incorporate all kinds of multimedia clips into your PowerPoint presentation to make it exciting and meaningful to your audience. Always beware of inflicting on them the infamous "Death by PowerPoint". Here are some golden rules for designing slides:

- Bullet points only
- No more than 5 short points per slide
- Keep each slide up for at least one minute and speak around it
- Large font size
- Plenty of white space
- Add colour, movement and sound for impact, but make sure...
- ... the message shines through and is not drowned by gimmicks

Ground Rules ☺ **Respect** ☺ **Listen** ☺ **Share**	**Ground Rules** **Care and Respect** – it is important to treat others as you would like to be treated. **Listen** – Only one person to speak at a time. We will make sure everyone gets their chance. **Share** – join in.
Better PowerPoint	Poor PowerPoint

PowerPoint is there as an aid to focus people's attention and to reinforce visually the key points – the bare bones – of your message. You will put the flesh on the bones, filling in the detail as you speak, providing examples or asking your audience to add their own ideas. PowerPoint cannot do the whole job for you. If you want to give a lot of detailed information, use a handout or show a DVD.

4. Flip Chart

Use the flipchart. As you introduce yourself to the group and talk about what is going to happen next, you can either write up key ground rules as you mention them or, if the group are comfortable, engage them in discussion about ground rules, and note these as they emerge.

Or you can prepare in advance a sheet which you can have on display as people come in, or covered until you are ready to reveal it as you speak. Make this colourful and bold, and your natural handwriting will add character and warmth, as long as it's clear and legible, using the same rules as for PowerPoint slides.

A flip chart may not look as professional as a PowerPoint presentation, and you may prefer to get things prepared in advance, but one of the beauties of using a flip chart is its flexibility and immediacy. You can write things up as people say them, which involves them in the process and values their contribution. It makes the point more strongly as you reinforce what has been said by writing it in real time.

5. A4 sheet or leaflet

Some trainers give each person a printed programme as they arrive at the session, which includes the session objective and maybe also something about the process (see our example). They'll find it useful to make notes on, and to refer to throughout the session. You can refer back to it, to remind people what you have covered and how each activity fits into the whole. The trainer presented this detailed programme at the first session and invited negotiation – the group fed back later that they valued the chance to amend it and choose what to focus on.

Developing a Career Plan

This course is for people who are not working or are not happy in their job. We hope you will go away with some new ideas and an action plan to make them happen.

9.30 Introductions
Objectives for the Day
Career Review

10.15 What is Important to You?
Goals and Values: Exercises to discover what you want from a job (and life)

11.15 What Can you Do?
Skills Audit: Identify your strongest points
Includes a practical exercise

12.45 Lunch

1.30 What do you want to do?
Interests Questionnaire to give you new job ideas

2.00 Identify some Job Goals
Research ideas and narrow down to a few career goals

2.30 Action Plan
Draw up a practical plan to help you reach your goals

3.15 Tea

3.30 Negotiated Session
Finish exercises. Individual research. 1:1 tutor support.

4.00 Closing Session
Questions, Sources of further help, Evaluation.

4.45 End

This will be an informal day. You will be able to ask questions and join in. The group will be small (12 people).

6. Pictures...

...can speak a thousand words. Remember your visual learners? Try to use images whenever you can, even if they are simple and home-made. There is a wide variety of images available online but you will need to check licence agreements before using them.

Discussion

1. Pair discussion

Ask the group to discuss in pairs what they want to get out of the session, then to feed back jointly to the whole group. Responding to each point as they make it, writing it up on the flip chart and asking the rest of the group to comment, will turn the contracting into a natural and inclusive activity rather than a long speech from you.

People usually learn more by doing than by listening or watching. Activists especially need to speak early in the session – they hate sitting and listening. Working in pairs also has the advantage of helping to break the ice – once a shy client has managed to talk to the person next to them, they will find it easier to carry on talking and gradually get brave enough to speak out in front of the group.

We often use a question to focus the group on the objectives – that way, we find out if we are likely to be meeting their needs, and we can adapt our programme if necessary.

Often in the early stages of a session, people are shy and lack confidence, so we ask them to discuss with the person next to them, and maybe to present the other person's answers. Typical questions are:

- What do you want to get from this session?
- What brought you here today?
- What do you already know about this subject?
- Have you any worries or concerns about today?

We keep a close eye on every pair as they discuss, to make sure everyone is involved. We also time-keep for them and remind them when it is time to swap over to let the other person speak.

We then lead them into the next stage, which is to go round the room hearing from each person. As they speak, we write a word or two on to the flip chart reflecting **every** point made. This values each person's input and helps everyone (including the trainer) focus on what has been said. As we write up the points we usually add a comment, always finding something positive to say, even if we have to add "sorry but we won't be covering that today".

We try to show a link between their wishes and the topics we have already planned to cover. We still keep an open mind in case our plan is really not going to meet most people's needs – we may need to re-negotiate (re-contract), or alter our timings.

The question about worries and concerns might lead us naturally into agreeing and contracting boundaries or ground rules.

2. Re-contracting

As well as re-negotiating the objectives and agenda, you may need to return to the ground rules if people start to break the rules they agreed to. If these have been written on the flip chart and stuck to the wall, it's easy to point to them and gently remind people.

Referring back to the contract also helps you show the group how they are progressing through the session as you planned it, which makes them feel good about themselves for achieving something, and reassures them that you are capable of managing the event to achieve your objectives.

3 Recall Prior Learning *and* Present New Learning

Now that you have agreed what the session is about, it is wise to find out how much people know about it already. No one wants to sit through a session that tells them nothing new. You are unlikely to get a group of people who are at exactly the same stage in their learning – this is one of the problems in a group situation that you don't get in one to one. By finding out at the earliest possible stage, at least you know the size of the problem and can decide how to tackle it.

The earliest possible stage is well before the day of the session. Some trainers make a point of phoning each attendee individually. They introduce themselves, ask what the person expects from the session and what they already know about the subject. While it is still important to remind people of their prior learning on the day, this phone call has numerous advantages. It begins to break the ice; it encourages the person to actually turn up; it gives you advance warning if they are likely to cause some storming (see Group Dynamics in Part Four); and you get a feel for what level to pitch your session.

If you are delivering your session to a group who already attend a centre, workplace, school or college, you can ask their support worker, manager or teacher what they've already covered and what they can cope with. These people may or may not give you much information, but it's always worth a try. You don't want to go in and deliver a session identical to the one they had last week. Nor do you want to prepare a lot of exercises way beyond or beneath their ability. Most of us have learned this lesson the hard way.

However much you have found out in advance, remember that people learn best when they can fit the new learning into a pattern or system that already exists in their heads. You need to start where they are at and build on it. So you find a way to get each person to recall what they know. How?

Toolkit for Recalling Prior Learning

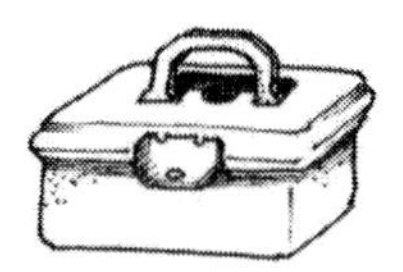

1. Questions – to the Whole Group

- CV's - What should a CV contain? How long should it be? How should it be presented? What should be left out?
- Choosing a Career – What have you already thought of? What made you think of that? What's important to you in a job?
- Interview skills – What do employers look for? How should you dress? What if you can't answer a question?

You can ask each question one at a time and let people call out their answers. Writing the question (and then their answers) on a flip chart will help them remember the discussion. As you go – or better, after everyone has said their piece – you can confirm or correct – this will now be the next step "Present New Learning". Remember to observe body language. Non verbal responses might give you vital information, for example a quiet person may be settling down because they realise the content is familiar to them and within their comfort zone - or they may be terrified, scared of being embarrassed because everyone else seems to know things that they don't.

2. Questions – to work on in Pairs or in Small Groups

Present them with the same questions as those above but ask them to discuss together first and then report back. This has several advantages. They have more time to think for themselves without relying on you to provide the information. Thinking and expressing their ideas to another person is active – they will learn from themselves and from each other – this is one way to cope with differing levels of prior learning – people often don't mind covering old ground if they are able to show (off) their knowledge to someone else. Working in pairs or very small groups means everyone is likely to get a chance to speak without having to sit and wait to go round the whole room. There is more of a buzz of activity and everyone is engaged. You create an interest in your topic when you present the new learning, because they want to check whether they got it right.

3. Questions about their feelings or their past experience

- What worries you most about job interviews?
- When's the last time you had an interview?

Both these questions will give you an idea where you need to pitch your input. If people have attended lots of interviews, some recently, they will know more than someone who has never attended one. From their descriptions, you'll get some idea of the kind of position they are going for, and where to pitch the new content you present.

4. Reminding them what they already know

Teachers throughout the ages have used examples from their audience's experience in their daily lives to help them understand new concepts. To help job seekers understand what employers are looking for at interview, we could ask them to remember what it feels like to recruit staff. Most people have never been in that position, so instead we ask them to imagine that they are looking for a hairdresser to come to their home to do their hair.

Each person has to imagine an evening when several hairdressers call in turn, and to think what might make them choose one rather than the others. Almost everyone can do this exercise – even if they don't have a hairdresser come to the house, most people have used the services of a hairdresser and know what they like and dislike. Just a reminder, however, that you need to think about the cultural background of your group members and make sure your examples are relevant to them.

We ask our job seekers to compare their list of criteria with another person's, then feed back jointly to the group. As we note their points, we link them to the new learning we want to present – in this case:

Employers are looking for three things:
Can you do the job?
Will you do the job?
Will you fit in?

This new learning will stick more effectively because each individual's own experience of thinking how they would select "an employee" has given them some understanding of how it feels to be an employer.

5. Recall a past feeling and recreate it

At job interviews, the first few seconds when you walk in the door are said to be crucial in forming an opinion in the mind of the interviewer that it's hard to shift whatever you say later in the interview. Some people find it hard to perform at their best at the start of an interview – they need time to warm up and relax. To help people make a good entrance, we can ask them to recall a time when they felt really confident and on top form. We might ask them to describe the good experience to the person next to them, or just to visualise themselves back in that situation. Then they can recall that situation and feeling later in the session when they are practising their entrance, and see what difference it makes to their performance.

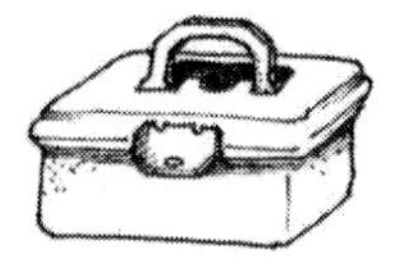

Toolkit for Presenting New Learning

At last, you can get on with the job and give them what they came for. This stage is equivalent to "Give Information to the Client" in one to one work. Your job here is to expose them to the new skills, facts or ideas, and also to offer some guidance to help them take these on board. Your methods may include:

1. Presentation (spoken, visual, written, audio-visual)
2. Demonstration (by you; or audio-visual – a tape or DVD)
3. Learning by doing – an activity

Remember the Confucius saying we have quoted before:

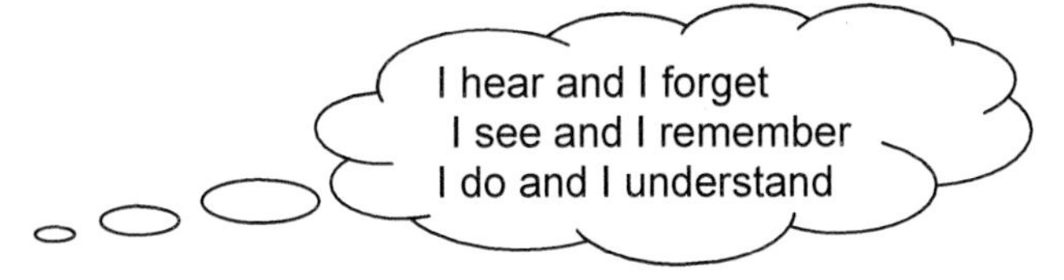

Also remember NLP's three types of learner – Auditory, Visual and Kinaesthetic (see Part Two). Whichever of these makes the most sense to you and fits with your experience of people, the suggestion is that a combination of all three methods of presenting information will achieve the best result for the greatest number of people.

1. Spoken Presentation

Traditionally, teaching meant someone standing at the front of the room talking to (at) us, giving us facts. Listening to a talk or lecture, watching a DVD, reading from a written page, these are all forms of learning by presentation. It is unlikely that you will conduct a whole session without doing some presenting – defining your objectives, perhaps, or giving information that your group need to know. Some people like presentations – theorists want the whole picture; they like to be told how it is by someone who has the relevant expertise.

Andrew Leigh and Michael Maynard give us the Five P's for "The Perfect Presentation" (Leigh & Maynard, 2003). Here is a summary of their ideas:

Preparation

- Research your audience
- Plan presentation and visual aids

Purpose

- Be sure what you want to achieve
- What is your message?

Presence

- Establish your presence before starting to speak: pause, stand confidently, breathe slowly and calmly, look around, make eye contact, smile
- Maintain interest by varying your facial expressions and body language, volume and speed of speech
- Be aware of what you and the audience can see, hear, smell, touch & feel around you in the room
- Don't distract by appearance/dress that is not in

		keeping with your message
	•	Avoid odd movements (gestures, nervous tics) and irritating noises (rattling loose change, over-repeated phrases)
Passion	•	People only learn if they want to, and people are moved by feelings. If you don't believe passionately in your message, why are you giving it? Get in touch with your feelings and show them to your audience
Personality	•	You don't have to turn into a TV presenter
	•	But the audience need to feel YOUR personality – if they can connect with a real live person, they will receive that person's message

Don't worry though – if you find it hard to stand up and speak for long, you don't have to. Some learners hate to sit still and listen, and will be only too pleased if you quickly move on to an exercise or discussion. Even theoretical learners will learn best from a variety of activities including doing or discussing as well as listening and thinking.

2. Video or DVD

A DVD can seem a good way to bring learning to life. It certainly has its place, especially if you want to show the group what goes on in environments they have no experience of. They can watch a surgical operation and see what the various professionals do; they can watch a job interview and see the impression the applicants make on the interviewers.

Too much sitting and watching a DVD is a waste of the potential of bringing a group together – they could do that at home, after all. If you use a DVD, it should be to stimulate discussion, or to present models for them to imitate. You should have a clear idea of what you will ask the participants to do afterwards and you need to tell them what to look out for.

If your group are watching a DVD showing three people being interviewed, you can:

- Ask them to work out who is going to get the job, and why (or why not).
- Stop the DVD fairly frequently to ask what they think.
- Tell them to note down one of the questions they see being asked, and afterwards to role play in pairs, using the same question.

PITCHING AND PACING

Julie: I went to a talk about keeping up to date with the internet, having the vague notion that this would helpfully contribute to my professional development.

I didn't learn a thing. The presenter used highly technical language, spoke at a fast pace, flashed through crowded, complicated slides and assumed his audience had a starting point that was well in excess of mine. Maybe some of them did understand, but for me, the information flew way over my head without stopping.

It's worth considering the impact it can have on confidence and self esteem if you feel totally out of your depth. It is wasting time at best, and soul destroying at worst. It's far better to grasp a little than be deluged with a vast weight of gobbledygook.

3. Demonstration – Learning by Watching

A DVD is a kind of demonstration but in our experience learners often prefer to watch real people, especially the "teacher" or facilitator, ie: you. This works especially well if you are demonstrating psycho-motor skills – how to make something, how to perform a sports technique, how to operate a machine. The learning will be limited though, unless they have a chance to imitate soon afterwards. If you offer advice in the area of learning and work, you can use demonstration to teach interview techniques, and interpersonal skills such as how to avoid conflict, how to be assertive in saying "no" or asking for what you want.

A risk in giving this kind of personal demonstration is that you might not do it perfectly. You may prefer to use a DVD, but remember that your group will prefer to watch you - we have often been asked "can we see you do it?" If you get it wrong, you can ask them to say what you did wrong, and how you could have done it better. By having the courage to get it wrong in public, you are modelling important social skills such as transparency, honesty and confidence by showing that it's OK to make mistakes. You will also model how to receive negative feedback as well as positive.

4. Learning by Doing – an Activity

Doing something will appeal to the activists in the group even more than being asked to discuss a problem or case study and come up with answers. Examples of activities we have used are:

Choose the best – this was an update on CV's for a group of experienced people with at least average literacy, who were facing redundancy after many years in the same job.

- You prepare six CV's of varying quality and length
- Put one copy of each in an envelope for each participant
- Tell them that apparently the average time a recruiter takes to look at a CV is 30 seconds

- Have a brief job description displayed on a PowerPoint or flip chart, or give it to them on paper
- Give them three minutes to shortlist the two best applicants for a given job
- Add pace by watching the clock and telling them when to open the envelope, when they have only a minute left, and when to stop
- Ask them which CV they chose, but don't dwell too long on this – go on to ask what made it easy to spot what they were looking for (good layout, a profile, bullet points, etc)
- Write these points up on the flip chart as they make them – allow for discussion between members as you go

Illustrate an image – this was for teaching young people who had never worked how to present themselves at interview.

- Give each person two A4 sheets each with a stick person on, plus a set of coloured pens
- Ask them to draw on one person clothes they should wear for the interview and on the other, "what not to wear"
- As they complete them, stick everyone's picture on the wall and ask them to come out in turn and describe what they have drawn

We found they greatly enjoyed designing the "NO" person, and were surprisingly conventional in how they dressed their "YES" person. Without realising it, each young person gave a mini presentation in front of the group. It turned into a great confidence builder – giving some witty and bright young people a chance to show what they could do.

Card sort and other rating exercises – this can be a practical way for people to think about what is important – to understand themselves and to prioritise. We've used it to help them work out what is most important to them in a job – their own feelings and values. We can also use it to help them avoid pitfalls, for example an in-tray exercise of phone calls, emails and other requests that they might face in a typical day at work, asking them what should be done first.

The advantage of presenting each item on a different card or piece of paper, as well as particularly appealing to people with visual and kinaesthetic (and active) learning styles, is that they can change their minds any number of times, and engage in discussion as they work, embedding the learning more deeply. There are a couple of excellent card sort exercises (about values and skills) in the workbook Build Your Own Rainbow (Hopson and Scally, 1999).

Another excellent visual paper exercise is Ayd Instone's version of the Wheel of Life, which he calls The Goal Chasm. This is a rating exercise to help identify and prioritise the areas of your life that need attention (downloadable from his website – see Bibliography).

Plan a project – this was a self-awareness "Know your strengths" exercise for a group of people hoping to return to work after a break. It works better in a longer session or course, where people have got to know each other a bit first – a one-day session would be sufficient.

- Get into groups of four or five, and plan a business that you could run between you.
- Using materials available in a children's playgroup, present your business to the rest of the group.

After they have learned by doing the planning and the presentation, you can reinforce the points you want them to take on board, through a short presentation. You might talk about different types of skill, showing how everyone has something to offer, and also linking their skills to careers and jobs. It can also help groups to appreciate each other and to bond.

Case Studies – although you could give these as individual exercises, you will make good use of the group situation if you ask people to discuss them in pairs or small groups.

- You can present the case as a written paragraph on paper, or a short DVD clip, often describing a person and their problem that needs to be solved.

- The group can either come up with solutions or simply identify the issues.
- If your objective is to raise their awareness of information resources and enable them to use these for themselves, you may provide access to information to help solve the problem.

Pragmatists will often enjoy case studies, provided they are relevant to their situation. Activists like to get involved, so researching and finding specific practical solutions will appeal to them.

Reviewing the activities and summarising key points

If you use activities as a way to present new skills or knowledge, you will probably follow them with a review of what people learned from the activity. Then you'll present the new learning, which may be a set of facts, a model to follow, or a full list of information resources to fill the gaps in the list they came up with. The value of getting them to do something before you present your information is that they are motivated to listen because their interest has already been aroused and they want to know the answer.

Here are some examples of ways we have provided a range of information about the topic of the session so that the group members can choose what they want:

- Leaflets on the same subject. If you have a mixed ability group you could have the same topic written about at different levels, e.g. a simplified version of how to write a CV targeted at adults with a learning difficulty alongside the regular leaflet.
- A range of prospectuses from different providers listing formal and informal learning opportunities.
- Web pages describing job roles that include photos both to break up the text and to give a feeling for the workplace involved.
- Printouts of home pages from different websites that show menus and tabs, so that they can see and discuss which sites might help them.

- Invite a visitor for them to question, or incorporate into our session a group visit to a workplace or a library where they can ask questions and seek out what they want.

As in your one to one work, when you present new information, do beware of the temptation to overload people. This is easy to do in your enthusiasm to meet every need and cover every angle, but it is highly likely to backfire. Useful, relevant information is easily lost if it is in a sea of handouts or slides. Remember "bite size chunks" (see Part Two).

Toolkit for Providing Learning Guidance

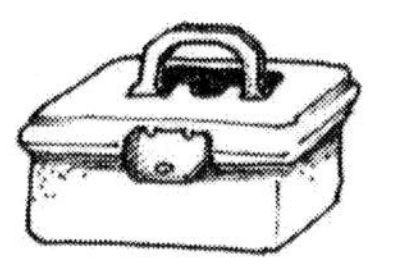

Learning guidance simply means helping people to grasp and remember what you have taught them. You will usually do this at the same time as you present the new information. Ways to help people understand and remember include:

1. Explain with an example

Follow up a general, theoretical statement with a specific example in a real time and place, with a real person. *For example:*

> *"Research tells us that people make judgements about us based less on what we say (only 7%) than the way that we say it (93%). For example, if the sales assistant at the checkout says 'Have a nice day' while glaring at you and slamming the till shut, you probably don't believe they mean it sincerely."*

Tell stories about real people, perhaps characters and events from well known films or TV shows:

"It's like what happened to xxx on EastEnders....."

– of course you will choose your film or programme to suit your particular audience's likely tastes, and make sure someone explains it to those who didn't see the show.

2. Bring in real examples

Give them case studies, copies of job adverts or application forms, pictures. If you are discussing suitable ways to dress for interview, you could have a set of photos either to hand out or to display on your PowerPoint. We often do a demonstration of performing at interview, perhaps inviting one of the group to give us a grilling.

3. A catchy phrase

Rhymes or mnemonics – SMART goals helps us remember they should be Specific, Measurable, Attractive*, Realistic and Time bound. *There are several views on what the A of SMART should stand for – you can choose what you like, and you can make up your own mnemonic to suit your purpose for the particular group you are working with.

The only things Ann remembers from a First Aid course done long ago is the order in which to tackle injuries:

"Breathing, Bleeding, Bones"

and that the best first aid treatment for burns is:

"Water, Water, Water".

These phrases were repeated over and over by the tutor until we couldn't forget them – and they may come in useful one day when panic drives out rational thought.

You could make up a rhyme – perhaps base it on a well known rhyme or even a song and set it to music.

4 Allow Performance *and* Provide Feedback

Only by performing will people know if they have learned anything – they must have a go. It may then be obvious to them how much they have moved forward but they may also need some feedback and guidance as to how to improve further.

You need to plan carefully to set up the opportunity for them to perform and receive feedback. Your role at this stage* is twofold:

- **stand back** and let them work independently - give them the time and space to reflect and experiment
- **keep watch** and be on hand to guide - you still need to make sure they use the time effectively and keep safe

*In Part Four we will see how groups pass through a number of stages in their life cycle: Forming, Storming, Norming and Performing. The idea is to develop your group through the first stages to a point where you can stand back and give them more freedom to practise what they have learned.

Toolkit for Allowing Performance

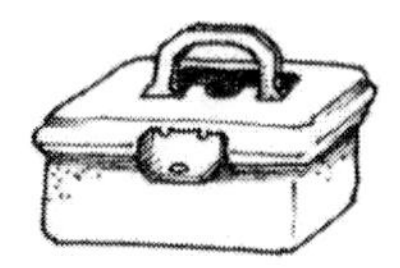

What you set up will depend very much on the time and space available to you. Here are some ideas:

1. Written exercises

The most traditional exercises are paper based. Having told people how to solve a mathematical problem or to use grammar and punctuation, you can set them some tasks or questions where they have to put the new learning into practice. If you are putting across factual information, you could give them sentences to complete or a crossword to solve.

2. Games

You might liven things up by devising board games or quizzes, to make it competitive. We've used an acronym quiz around Christmas time – people have to show what they have learned about legislation, organisations and initiatives in Advice and Guidance (a fairly dry topic). We give them a list of initials (IAG, LSC, NVQ...). They have to work in pairs and say what they initials stand for *and also* invent a Christmas-related phrase using the same initials. They are awarded one sweet for each right answer and another for the pair who invent the funniest Christmas phrase for each acronym.

You can also make competitions out of many of the exercises we have mentioned, by dividing the group into teams to race against each other on a task. We have made competitions out of quizzes, construction tasks (for example building a model with a children's construction kit following spoken instructions from a team member – to learn how to give information clearly) and creative activities around generating ideas or problem solving.

3. Try it out for real

If you are teaching people to ride a bike, the performance stage has to involve getting on that bike and riding it. The same goes for making presentations, writing on the flip chart, baking a cake, doing a new dance step or laying bricks.

In guidance for learning and work, trying it out for real may have to take place at a different time, although some things can be done in the session. You can ask them to write part of their CV – for example their profile – and have time to do this and receive feedback. There is often time to draft a letter or devise an action plan to job seek more effectively. They can try out the first five minutes of a presentation to the rest of the group, even if they will not have time to do the whole thing. We have had had groups of jobseekers prepare for a phone call, actually go into the room next door and make the call, then report back to the group on how it went.

Doing it For Real

During a session of a Return to Work course for people who had not worked for several years, Malcolm made a phone call.

The course had already covered the benefits of having a job, how to overcome obstacles, what type of job is right for you and where to look. Malcolm, it transpired, had always been frightened of employment, with a strong set of incorrect assumptions firmly embedded. The group leader can't take all the credit for his change of attitude - hearing his fellow group members talking about jobs they had in the past contributed greatly.

A penny dropped and Malcolm decided that a job would be a good idea, as long as he could work outside. He rang a friend who worked for a landscaping company. They needed someone. He hadn't been employed for a very long time, but was quite handy in the home and garden, with skills to offer. He went for an interview the next day and got the job.

4. Role Play

This could be the next best thing if it is not practical for them to do it for real. People are not always keen on role play. At our interview skills courses, we found that the promise of a role play started immediate panic among at least half the group members (reflectors in particular), so we tend to use the expression "skills practice" instead.

While we don't like frightening people – it's not the best way to create a friendly, encouraging atmosphere – we believe that some things can only be learned in the same way as you learn to drive. You can listen to the theory and watch a demonstration, but unless you have a go, you will never be able to drive that car. If you are helping people to perform better at interview, make a presentation, deal with an argument between two children, respond assertively to a bullying boss, or write clearly on a flip chart, you will sell them short if they go away from your session without having had a go and received some feedback.

You can make the experience less painful, however. In our interview techniques courses, we build them up gently:

- We get people first to work in pairs, each asking the other just one question and letting them practise answering it, then swopping roles. It's very low key, no one else is watching, and the embarrassment potential is kept to a minimum.
- Once this is completed, we move them on to working in threes, with one person taking the role of observer.
- We agree timings, so that each person can have a go in each role – say five minutes for each "interview" followed by five minutes evaluation and feedback, before changing roles and starting again. This requires at least 30 minutes for the role play session, plus ten minutes at the end for a whole group review of the experience.

Our role as facilitators of role play is to make sure we have given clear instructions and set clear boundaries (especially about how to feed back) and then to keep out of the process except to keep a discreet eye on proceedings, intervening only if a group is straying too far from the ground rules or time boundaries. If we are the only facilitator, it's best to keep them all in one room but far enough away from each other not to be distracted by what's happening in another threesome.

We keep at equal distance from each threesome, probably wandering round sharing ourselves equally between each, but not getting involved unless it is obvious they have forgotten time boundaries or they are clearly wandering away from the brief. We sometimes have to remind them to stay in role, for example, or to be gentle with each other. Every ten minutes, we might say *"you should all be getting to the second / third interview by now".*

If they are working in three's, with one of them playing the role of observer, it is helpful to give the observer a sheet with hints of what to look for/comment on. People often struggle with the concept of giving feedback, and slip into the default position of saying everything was OK, which isn't very helpful. Using an observation sheet helps them know what to look for, gives some structure to their feedback and can also be taken away by the person they are observing. Here are some ideas for content on an observation handout:

- What body language did you see? Was it effective?
- What types of questions were used?
- How was the pace and tone of voice?
- What worked well?
- What did not work well? Why not?
- Any suggestions for a different approach?

Role play debrief – After the role play is completed, it is very important to debrief properly by asking the whole group how they felt about the exercise, and making sure that no one has been upset by it. It is important to congratulate them on the risk they have taken and how well they did, thanking them for supporting each other too.

"McMaster" Role Play

No one can tell us who McMaster is or was, but this method seems to be well known. You organise the role play so that three or four members can share the load and play the role of one person. Let them discuss the preparation, and then decide who goes first. It works like this - the player who has been selected to go first starts off the role play. At any point either they, or any one else in their team, can call "Time out!" and the role play pauses. Give them a strict time – usually a minute – to consult each other. They may choose to feed the player lines if someone has had an idea of how to handle the situation, or they can swap and let someone else pick up the mantle and take over the role play. This is an effective training method as it relieves the pressure by providing a get-out clause. Also, those who shy away from role play can get involved without having to be in the spotlight.

5. Respond to case studies

We have already suggested case studies as a way of drawing on people's prior experience. You can also use them as a way for people to put into practice the new principles that you have brought to them or to apply new information. Some examples – if you have discussed:

- **New sources of information on job opportunities** – give them a case study describing a person and their previous experience, then ask them to use the sources to locate jobs for that person
- **How to respond to aggressive people** – give them a case study describing a scenario and ask them to suggest what the person should do
- **How to adapt their dress to different types of employment** – give them a few case studies describing places of work and ask them to suggest suitable outfits
- **There are different places and study modes for the same kind of training** – give them case studies of people like them but with differing personal circumstances (mum with children; person at work all day; someone who finds reading difficult; person who does not like big groups) plus lists of courses and ask them to find the best course for each.

People could respond to a case study individually, either in writing or by telling you or a small group what they would do. They may learn more by working on it in small groups, to first reach agreement amongst themselves and then choose a spokesperson to report back to the full group.

6. Produce something

Make an item (object, leaflet, presentation) in groups or individually – making something can be a hands-on way to show what you have learned. Here's a random selection of things to make related to IAG for learning and work:

- Illustrated instruction leaflet eg: "How to do well at interviews"
- Personal sales leaflet listing your five key qualities
- Poster or Banner – illustrate and list a set of "golden rules" or a message for how to behave in certain situations, eg interviews:

  "head up – shoulders back – eye contact – smile"

- Decorate a T-shirt with slogan praising your qualities, eg:

  "Cool under Pressure" *"Friendly and Reliable"*

  "I'm a People Person"

- Make up a mnemonic, poem, even a song or a mini-play to illustrate a point. In interview workshops (see session plan on pages 164-5) we use the acronym STAR to help people answer interview questions about their skills and experience. In this order they describe:

  S*ituation*

  T*ask*

  A*ction*

  R*esult*

- Your group can make up their own mnemonic for a key idea, eg:

  C.....................
  O.....................
  N.....................
  F.....................
  I......................
  D.....................
  E.....................
  N.....................
  C.....................
  E.....................

Toolkit for Providing Feedback

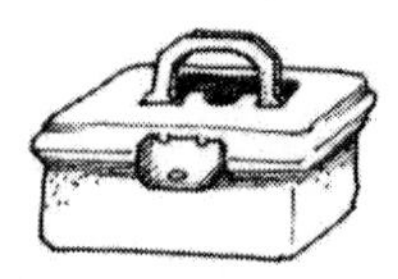

In Part Two we give you the golden rules of giving feedback, so if you are planning activities and wondering how best to give feedback, please make sure you understand the basics before trying any of our suggestions.

1. Responding to Learners

For most (though not all) people, speaking out in front of the group, especially for the first time, will be nerve wracking. It is very important that you respond warmly, positively and encouragingly, even if their input is way off track (unless it is deliberately offensive to another group member). Remember the Feedback Sandwich? Respond in three stages:

Positive

"Thank you John for that, I can see what you mean..."
"Mmm, that's an interesting idea..."
"A good try, John, well done..."
"Thanks for setting the ball rolling..."

But...

"It's not quite what I meant"
"Possibly in another situation, but in this case..."
"Let's see – what do other people think – any other ideas?"

Positive

"However, I would like to come back to your idea in a minute; I'll note it on the flip chart"
"It was a good try, though, well done"
"This was the first time you've spoken out in front of the whole group – you did brilliantly!"

If you don't notice someone (especially the quieter members) when they try to speak, they may interpret this as negative feedback. You need to be alert, especially to the quieter people in the group. They may not want the limelight, but you can find ways of showing them approval even if the others don't hear it – eye contact, a smile and a nod or a thumbs-up can suffice. Writing someone's idea on the flip chart – perhaps with their name beside it – is another way to show you value their input. There are tips on handling the silent ones in Part Four.

2. Planning to give Feedback on Performance

If you have set up the opportunity to perform, to try it for real or to simulate in a role play, you need to think ahead about how you will give feedback. You could use:

- Self assessment
- Peer feedback
- Group leader feedback
- Assessment

Self assessment – with some activities it is immediately evident whether the person has succeeded or not – riding a bike is an obvious example. However, if they fall off, or only manage a few metres before stopping, they may assume they have performed worse than they have, and they need you to tell them or help them work out what they did right and what they need to change.

Some models of coaching now focus on helping the person work out for themselves by catching them doing something right and encouraging them to focus on that moment and recall what they were thinking and feeling in that moment, then try to reproduce it.

You can encourage people to self assess, perhaps first helping them draw up a checklist to assess themselves against. We use this in interview coaching for people to use after every interview they attend in future. You can also give out a form at the end of the session for them to note what they have achieved and what they need to develop further.

Peer feedback – you can plan peer feedback into the activities you set up, especially role plays with an observer. Even without an observer, you can ask the other person in a pair how it felt for them being on the receiving end. We mentioned above that in role plays we usually provide a feedback checklist for observers to use. Better still, make the drawing up of the checklist one of your exercises – in small groups they can decide what they will look for and then they can produce their own checklist.

We use peer feedback at the Ending stage of a session (or course of sessions). This aims to contribute to the "mourning" part of "adjourning" in the group process (see Part Four) – not so necessary after a single one-hour or half-day session, but important if a group have bonded over time. Even after a short session, if confidence building and social skills are included in our learning objectives, peer feedback has a strong part to play. Some activities we use are described in the section on Ending.

Feedback from you, the group leader or facilitator – we have already shown that you are providing informal feedback as soon as you start interacting with your group. If you set up the opportunity for them to perform, whether it's answering written or oral questions, taking part in a presentation or role play, making something or performing a physical feat, you will need to tell them what they did well, what they could do better and how to improve further.

We have already discussed the feedback sandwich and the coaching approach which places as much of the assessment as possible on the individual themselves. If you use the coaching approach, do not mistake this for a cop-out on your part – you will be enabling this self assessment and ensuring it is realistic, not just dodging the difficult task of giving feedback.

Assessment - Assessment sounds and is more formal than feedback. If people need some kind of certification, you might have to provide what is known as summative assessment – a final judgement as to whether their performance is sufficient to meet the standard required to achieve the certificate. This is unlikely in a one session groupwork event, and will not be covered in this book, as it is a subject in its own right.

The other kind of assessment is known as formative, and its purpose is to enable people to develop and increase their skills. The feedback you provide on their performance will help them if you tell them what they did well, what could be improved and specifically what action they can take to improve. This should be private between you and the individual and can be offered in speech or in writing. You will want to decide in advance whether you are going to offer this kind of assessment and inform the group at the start when and how you will provide it.

3. How to say "Well Done!"

On the next page is our list of 30 ways to say "Well Done!" with space for you to add your own favourite phrases.

Of course, you can express positive feedback in other ways besides verbal. It is hard to describe non verbal behaviour here, but can you think of body language that expresses approval? Think if the continental action of kissing (your own!) finger and thumb when something is very good, or the power of an open handed gesture accompanied by a smile and a raise of the eyebrows, or a pat on the back. What is it that you do when you approve?

Other things you can do to give feedback and reinforce positive behaviour or learning fall into the category of rewards. For example:

- Smile, exclamation, applause
- Chocolate balls/coins thrown when a good point is made
- Paper rosette, gold star
- Doughnuts, biscuits, jelly babies
- Impromptu awards - Group Head of Creative Thinking, Master of Problem Solving, Most Friendly Team Member, Most Cheerful Group Member.....

4. Thirty ways to say "Well done!"

Our list	You add your own...
• Well done! • Beautiful work • I'm very proud of you • That's great • Cool • Wow! • You've done this before • You've been practising • Jo made a good point there • Thank you • *smile and nod* • *thumbs up* • I like that • I like the way you.... • Good • Yes • I'm liking it • Excellent! • Now, that's good..... • I'm impressed! • I wish I'd thought of that • You've got it! • What an improvement • Bravo! • Congratulations • Good for you • You haven't missed a thing! • Nice one • That's much, much better • Fantastic!	☺ .... ✓ .... ★ .... ☑ .... 👍 .... ☑ .... ☆ .... ☺ .... ✓ .... ★ .... ☑ .... 👍 .... ☺ ....

5 Evaluate Learning *and* Prepare for Ending

Endings are as important as first impressions in influencing how people will feel about your session and how much it will help them.

In one-to-one work, we know that people remember most strongly the first experience they have of you and, almost as strongly, the last. So you want them to go away feeling good about the session and able to use what you have given them. Presenters have a saying:

1. Tell them what you are going to tell them
2. Tell them
3. Tell them what you have told them

You are now at the third stage, and summing up the issues learned in order to reinforce them one last time. We have quoted Confucius before:

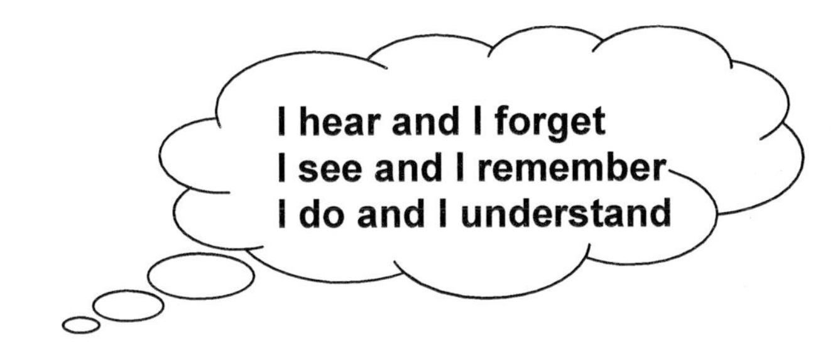

Rather than tell them (they will simply hear it), why not ask them to tell you what they have gained? This will serve as feedback from them to you, but will also, more importantly, fix it in their minds.

Reviewing what they have learned will be part of evaluating your session. Who is evaluation for? There are three distinct sets of stakeholders in this session that you are running:

- **The group members** – evaluation will help reinforce what they have learned so that it can be more useful to them in their lives. It will also contribute to the ending process for them, providing a sense of wellbeing through understanding how they have spent the time and how it was valuable to them.
- **You as facilitator or session leader** – you need to know how effective your work has been, partly for your own satisfaction and also to inform your planning of any future sessions – your continuing professional development.
- **The funders** – someone has paid for this session and they want to know if it was money well spent. They will have had a purpose in mind, and they will want to know if the session delivered.

In the field of learning and development, evaluation is seen to work at four levels:

- **Reaction** – How do the participants feel immediately after the session? How good was the experience for them? Did they enjoy it? Was it interesting? Did they like the facilitator (you) and your methods? Did they feel comfortable in the group?
- **Learning** – Have they learned anything new? Did they get what they came for? Can they do anything they could not do before?
- **Applied Learning** – What will this learning do for them? Will they be able to use it to improve their performance at work, to manage their lives better or simply to get more from life?
- **Results** – How will this learning benefit the wider world? How will it benefit society, their community, the economy, their employer, their children?

The time to think about these points is actually at the very start, when you plan your session and define your objectives, which can now be used at this evaluation stage to measure the effectiveness of your work.

Toolkit for Evaluating the Session

The Questions

What you ask will depend on what you want to find out. Knowing that evaluation can benefit different kinds of people and can be used for different purposes gives you options for the design of the questions you ask.

To Reinforce Learning for Participants so that it will be of real use to them, you can ask:

- What did you learn today?
- What did you get from this session?
- What was most useful about this session?
- How can you use what you learned today?
- What can you do differently after today?
- Name one action you will take following today's session and state when you will do it
- Name one way that you can use what you learned today.
- What kind of person would benefit from attending this session?

Some groups find it easier if you take the half finished sentence approach, asking them to complete things like:

- Today I have learned......
- What I want to do next is......
- How I will do this is........
- I will complete this by......
- I will get support from........
- I will know when I have done it because.....
- I now know..... I now feel..... Now I will be able to.....

To get Feedback to help you plan future sessions and/or your own development, you can ask:

- Please rate this session 1-5 for ... *enjoyment, interest, meeting your objectives, the tutor, the activities, the teaching methods, the venue, the refreshments, the arrangements*
- How much did you enjoy this session? What did you enjoy most?
- How useful was this session? What was most useful?
- What were your objectives for this session? Rate each 1-5 for how far it was met.
- Would you recommend it to others? If so, who and why?
- What did you get from today's session?
- What do you think should be done differently in future sessions?
- Complete these sentences:

  I liked....... I did not like...........

To get Feedback for Funders

Funders may actually prefer to evaluate sessions through observable, measurable results that may not be evident till later, such as:

- How many participants got a job, and how soon?
- How many people passed a test or exam?
- Did a department's productivity, quality or sales increase?
- Did people's behaviour change – fewer arguments, more enthusiasm, happier?

Funders may also be interested in participants' immediate reactions, if part of their purpose was to please them. You can give out a "happy sheet" or feedback form to be completed before they leave.

If you want to show immediate results in terms of learning, you could give a test to the group at the end of the session and as well as giving them their results, show them to those who have funded the session.

Toolkit for Getting the Answers

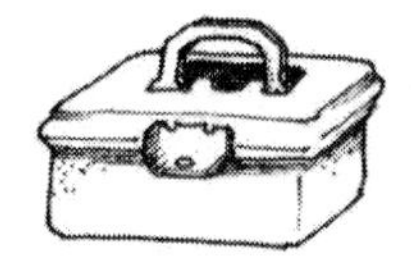

Forms – Feedback forms, Happy Sheets, Smiley Faces. These are useful evidence, especially for keeping funders satisfied and also to help you evaluate and plan for future work and your own development.

If you are using forms to help reinforce participants' learning, they must be able to take them away with them. In that case, how will you get access to the information on the form? You will need to be clear in your own mind, from the beginning, what information you need to keep for your evaluation, and what you want your group members to take away with them. If there is an overlap, make sure there is a photocopier to hand. Please try to avoid making them write the same information twice! On pages 152-3 there are examples of evaluation forms (feedback for you) and on page 155 a development plan (for the individual's own use).

Open or Closed Questions, Rating or Scaling – As you know from one to one work, open questions will get more meaningful answers, showing you what people really think, and can give you ideas you had not thought of. Closed questions, especially with rating or scaling, will give you figures that can be quickly and easily used in a report (*nine out of ten women between the ages of 20 and 50 prefer xxxx face cream.... 99% of participants were happy or very happy...*). Closed questions will only get answers to the questions you thought to ask, and you may never know what they would have preferred, or why they didn't like it. There is a place for both types of question in an evaluation.

Group Discussion – If you have plenty of time, you can either give the questions on paper, or write them on a flip chart or board, or have them on a PowerPoint slide. Ask the group to discuss them in pairs, small groups or as a whole group. Pairs and small groups can then report back to the whole group. During the whole group (plenary) discussion, you will facilitate and maybe prompt to encourage more exploration. The downside of this approach is that it is likely that they will agree with each other. If one member has a different view, they may not dare to speak out against the crowd and the most forceful person's view is the one we hear. We have found it is best to be present and facilitate this discussion rather than tactfully leave them to it, for this reason. Again, we can demonstrate our ability to respond to feedback – both positive and negative.

Sticky Notes – We have used these if we are short of time or if we know participants will be put off by yet another form to fill in. You can buy colourful sticky notes in various shapes (hearts, flowers, stars, arrows, speech bubbles) or just use the standard square ones. We give one or more to each person and casually tell them to write any short comment they like about how they feel – what they enjoyed or how we could improve. They stick them on our table on their way out.

Delayed Feedback – Send out evaluation forms one or more weeks after the event, to find out what lasting effect it had. Alternatively, either you or another person can ring or email each participant to find out how they feel later and whether anything has changed for them.

Usually you will tailor your evaluation form to meet your own requirements, or sometimes you might be provided with one. It is good to use a variety of methods of getting information, for example using open and closed questions plus rating scales.

In case you are starting from scratch, here are some examples we have used – we have attempted to adapt to different audiences:

Was the session fun? ☹ 😐 ☺

Did you learn something new? ☹ 😐 ☺

Any comments?..

....

PLEASE, tell us what you think...

This form is to help improve our services.

What did you **like most** about the course?

What did you **like least** about the course?

What have you **learned**?

How can you **use** what you have learned?

How do you think the course could be **improved**?

Thank you.

Evaluation Form

To help us continually improve, we would be glad of your feedback.

Did the training meet its stated objectives? Yes / No

What was your overall impression of session?

Which was the most useful part of the session?

Which was the least useful part of the session?

Please rate on a scale of 1 to 5 (1 is poor, 5 is excellent)

Facilitator's style	1	2	3	4	5
Materials (slides, handouts)	1	2	3	4	5
Course Organisation	1	2	3	4	5
How relevant was the session to you?	1	2	3	4	5

Any other comments?

6 Plan Next Steps *and* Say Good Bye

The final stage of your group session has to allow for one remaining task to be done and also for completion of the process of working together.

All models of guidance provide for a "plan next steps" stage. Egan's three-stage model ends with "Strategies for getting there". Ali & Graham's four-stage model ends with "Goals and Action". Bedford's seven-stage model gives us "Clarify Next Steps". Part One shows how closely Bedford's model for one-to-one work matches Gagné's nine stages of learning, on which we base this model for groupwork. Both one to one guidance and groupwork need to provide the participant with a means of putting into practice what they have gained from the session.

Toolkit for Planning Next Steps

Evaluation

You might combine this planning activity with the evaluation that you used in the previous stage. The questions "how will you use what you have learned?" and "what will you do as a result of today?" lead to an action plan. It's also fine for them to plan their next steps before they evaluate, because both are part of a process of coming a conclusion.

Group Discussion

You can broaden people's ideas for action by encouraging them to listen to each other's ideas before deciding what they will do. Group discussion will be more effective if it doesn't end there, but leads to each individual stating what he or she is going to do. This does not have to be written down, but if it is, the piece of paper will act as a reminder.

Action Plan Form

Providing a form to write the plan on, especially if it is attractive, can help to ensure the plan is kept, remembered and revisited (and hopefully acted upon). Here is an example of one we have used:

DEVELOPMENT PLAN

From today, areas I would like to improve upon are:

-
-
-

How I will practise my skills:

-
-
-

Situations in which I will act differently are:

-
-
-

Outcomes I am looking to achieve are:

-
-
-

How I will get support for my ongoing development:

Signed .... Date ....

Short and Long Term Goals

You can use visual images to give the idea of how the steps of a plan fit together and lead to a long term goal. Some ideas people have used involve:

- **Climbing up steps or a ladder** – with an action and time on each step
- **Flowchart –** boxes and arrows, often moving from left to right, showing options for different routes
- **Route map** – you could use a flowchart as above, or draw something that looks like a road map or Underground plan

Timeline

For people who learn better visually or kinaesthetically, you can demonstrate (and if there's enough time and space, encourage them to draw out or act out) the line from where they are now to where they want to be.

Done on paper, it is a simple line across the page, with a beginning point (where you are now) and an end point (where you want to be). The person marks along the line the actions that need to be taken and in what order, perhaps with dates beside them.

Taking this to the kinaesthetic level, the person places an object (chair, jumper, coloured ring, anything) at each end of an imaginary line, then places objects along it representing each action they need to take. They then stand at the beginning (now) and walk from object to object, stopping at each to describe (using the present tense) what they are doing. When they have completed this stage, they move on to the next object (action) and hopefully reach their goal at the end. This is an interesting exercise to try in one to one work also, where it can reveal some remarkable information about people's barriers, as well as making their goal more realistic and appealing. You can read more about walking a timeline in Angus McLeod's book on coaching (McLeod, 2003).

Saying Good-Bye

Adjourning

If people have spent time together, especially if they have been stretching themselves outside their usual comfort zone, putting themselves at risk by meeting new people and attempting new skills in an unfamiliar environment, they will have made an emotional investment in the experience. Adjourning is the last stage in the group process (see Part Four) and although it is often avoided or rushed, it is always emotionally beneficial to make time for a celebration of what you have had and a recognition that if it was good, there will be a need for some kind of mourning for what is now ending.

While this may sound over-dramatic and unnecessary for a short group session on how to write a CV, it is true that people usually seek to go through some kind of ritual for most endings. A week's holiday will have a last night get-together; a meal at a friend's will close with thanks and plans to meet again. We believe it is important to include some activity that is not strictly task-focused "business", even if the whole thing lasts only five minutes. In no particular order, think how you can enable people to:

- Express thanks
- Celebrate
- Mourn the ending
- Look forward
- Keep in touch
- Access further help

Toolkit for Saying Good-Bye

Presentation

You can take more control of this final part of your session and bring people together. Before the good-byes you can present a summary of what has been covered, and of what they can do next to continue their development and their own particular career journey. You might include how they can get further help if today has raised questions or other issues.

Ritual

Ritual helps us deal with emotionally difficult situations by providing something safe to hold and protect us while we experience and express unfamiliar feelings. We ran one year-long course where people said they hated the idea of being presented with a prize or certificate at the end, so we decided not to hold this ceremony. They then told us they were disappointed that there was no presentation. We concluded that ceremony and ritual might seem pompous or scary, but most of us still do like to use them to celebrate important moments.

Low-key equivalents to a prize-giving ceremony might be:

- With the group sitting in a circle or horseshoe, give out a certificate, a pack, a book, a sweet, (anything that could be a prize) to each person, addressing them by name and saying almost the same thing to each of them – "Well done, Ann, for .... today" – if you know them well enough and you can think of something equally positive to say about each.
- Ask group members to write on a sticky note something they have enjoyed about working in this group, then take each person's in turn, reading it out as you put arrange it on the board/wall/flipchart for all to see later.
- If you have very little time, you can simply make sure that everyone is sitting still and paying attention while you thank them

for their contribution during the session and wish them good luck for the future.

- If you have more time, with a group that has met several times, they can contribute more to the ending, perhaps bringing food to share. We'd leave at least half an hour at the end for this party.
- We have handed out sheets of paper each with one person's name on, and passed them round so everyone writes something they have liked or admired about that person, then presented everyone with their own sheet.
- A variation on this theme is passing round envelopes that contain a small piece of paper with each person's name on. Everyone writes on each piece of paper in the envelope they were given. When everyone one is done, each one takes an envelope and collects the slips written about them, so that they get an envelope full of positivity to take away with them.

Your Session Plan

How you actually write down your session plan will depend on a couple of things. Your own personal style will influence you, as will your level of confidence and experience. It's important to choose a format that suits you; it needs to be easy for you to follow and give you sufficient information to run the session smoothly – you will have it beside you in the session to remind you where are you and what to do next.

Ann prefers to use a table, based on the example on the next page. She finds it useful to run her eye down the "materials" column as she leaves the office, to make sure she's got everything she needs. Julie prefers just to list times and activities in a more freeform manner. We'll give you three examples of each to set you on your way, so that you can explore what suits you best.

Of course, there are other approaches. Some people use a stack of postcards with one activity and its timings on each. When one activity is over, they put that card to the back of the pack and move on to the next.

Another approach which works well, especially if you are not sure how long activities will take, or how experienced your group will be, is to colour code the programme:

- 'Must do' in black
- 'Should do' in red
- 'Could do' in green

This gives you the option of including or leaving out activities depending on how the session is going, but without losing the thread.

First, here is a blank table you could use or adapt to plan your session. Above the table, we would put the session title, venue and time, followed by the aim and objectives.

<table>
<tr><td colspan="2">Session Title</td><td colspan="2"></td></tr>
<tr><td colspan="2">Venue</td><td colspan="2">Time</td></tr>
<tr><td colspan="4">Aim</td></tr>
<tr><td colspan="4">Objectives – By the end of this session, participants will:
•
•
•</td></tr>
<tr><td>Stage</td><td>Timing</td><td>Activity</td><td>Materials & Equipment</td></tr>
<tr><td>Ice breaker Focus attention</td><td></td><td></td><td></td></tr>
<tr><td>Agree objectives and ground rules</td><td></td><td></td><td></td></tr>
<tr><td>Recall prior learning</td><td></td><td></td><td></td></tr>
<tr><td>Present new learning</td><td></td><td></td><td></td></tr>
<tr><td>Perform</td><td></td><td></td><td></td></tr>
<tr><td>Feed back</td><td></td><td></td><td></td></tr>
<tr><td>Evaluate</td><td></td><td></td><td></td></tr>
<tr><td>Plan next steps</td><td></td><td></td><td></td></tr>
<tr><td>Good bye</td><td></td><td></td><td></td></tr>
</table>

Example Session Plans

Over the next few pages, we have included six session plans to show you how we plan sessions. Three are in Ann's style (in tables, more thorough and detailed), and the other three in Julie's (more of a checklist with timings, with bold to highlight what's needed).

We hope these make sense to you – we haven't tidied them up to impress you. Most of them are real working documents for our own use only – until now! We hope they'll help you to plan your own sessions by adapting them to suit your purposes. They are plans for these sessions:

1. **Options at 16+**
   For a small group of 9-12 school students in year 11

2. **Do better in Job Interviews** (half day)
   Open to all, advertised publicly, held monthly in the local library

3. **CV Workshop** (half day)
   For staff facing redundancy

4. **It's Never Too Late to Change Career** (half day)
   For self employed people whose businesses had been wound up

5. **Winning Respect and Recognition** (one and a half hours)
   A workshop for administrative staff as part of a day long conference

6. **Assertiveness** (one and a half hours)
   A lunchtime workshop for employees in a housing organisation

Session Title *Options at 16+ - for year 11's*			
Venue *West Park School*		**Time** *11 – 11.50*	
Aim *Raise awareness of full range of options available to them and my role as guidance adviser*			
Objectives – By the end of this session, participants will: • *MUST Know the 3 main options – 6th form, work, college* • *SHOULD know options at each level – academic + vocational* • *SHOULD know at least one option to suit their own interests* • *MUST know they can book a 1:1 with me*			
Stage	**Time**	**Activity**	**Materials & Equipment**
Ice breaker Focus	11.00	Who am I? Discuss in pairs then tell me – respond to their answers	PowerPoint
Agree objectives, ground rules	11.10	Refer to title of workshop – ask what they want – check and agree – tell them my objectives	Flipchart and pens
Recall prior learning	11.15	Who do they know who left school in last 2 yrs – what are they doing?	Write their ideas on flip chart
Present new learning	11.25	3 options – school, college, apprenticeship; 4 levels – link to their *eg's*	PowerPoint Course leaflets
Perform	11.30	Give out bingo cards – give one *eg* to fill each box	Bingo cards Course leaflets
Feed back	11.35	Ask for answers – give out choc coin for each box filled correctly	Choc coins
Evaluate	11.40	Ask for volunteers to say one thing they've learned today	
Plan next steps	11.45	Each person to write down one thing to find out more about	Post-its
Good bye	11.49	Thank them. Tell them how to book appt with me	My card

COURSE: Do Better in Job Interviews 3 hours 12 people

OBJECTIVES:-By the end of the session students will:

1. Have analysed a job vacancy and matched their competencies to those required
2. Have practised describing their relevant competencies in a mock interview
3. Feel more confident in their ability to do well in a job interview

Time	Activities / Content	Delivery Method	Equip-ment	Materials
9.30	Introductions + Domestics Ground Rules & Issues Programme for morning	Present to whole group - invite participa-tion	Flip Chart Powerpt and Projector	Booklets P-point Slides 1-5
9.40	Ice breaker – Intro: What do you expect or fear from interviews?	Pair work, report back to whole gp	Flip chart	pens
9.55	What employers are looking for How interviews are structured and assessed	Present to whole group with questions	Projector	P-point Slides 6-9
10.00	Competency based interviews (1) Analyse a Vacancy and (2)give evidence - "STAR stories"	(1) Small groups then report back (2) whole group	Flip Chart	Example of a vacancy - 1 each Slide 10 STAR chart – 1 each Slide 11

continues on next page....

....continued from previous page

Time	**Activities / Content**	**Delivery Method**	**Equip-ment**	**Materials**
10.20	Analyse own vacancy and note own "STAR stories": Choose an incident: Describe Situation, Task, Actions taken, Result.	Individual work Facilitator help where needed		a Job Vacancy - provided by participants (have newspaper in case forgotten) STAR Chart
10.30	Practise describing orally one competency via a "STAR story"	Pairs, in turns – Monitor timing		
10.45	**B R**	**E**	**A**	**K**
11.00	Watch DVD	Breaks where indicated to discuss points	DVD player	DVD: *Against All Odds*
11.30	Interview Role Play and Observer Feedback	Groups of 3, in turns 15 mins each	Space to break into groups	Observation feedback checklist
12.15	Debrief issues and questions Write action plans	Whole Group		Action plan form Evaluation forms
12.30	**E**	**N**	**D**	

CV Workshop for Employees facing Redundancy 3 hours

Aims

- To give delegates sufficient knowledge and understanding to be able to construct an effective CV and personal statement
- To get them started on producing one of each
- To give delegates an overview of jobsearch techniques and methods

9.30am: Aims, programme, each other.
What do you want from today? Any concerns?
PowerPoint slides 1-6. Discuss in small groups,

9.45am flipchart responses, **PowerPoint slides 7-12**

10.10am Profile Exercise
Input – importance of the 'headline' etc, look at example profiles on **PowerPoint.**

Refer to **CV words handout.**
Work individually for 15 mins to brainstorm ideas, choose words you want to include in your profile, key skills etc. Move into pairs for 5 mins to get another persons opinion

10.40am Employment History
Eg on **PowerPoint**. Pulling out *relevant* key achievements, responsibilities, duties etc

11-11.15am coffee break

11.15am Example CV's
Show examples, look at critically. What impression do they create? (30 seconds is average looking time)
Different styles – skills based, functional etc
Clean layout, use of vocab etc
Questions on CV's?

cont'd on next page...

...cont'd from previous page

11.30am Application forms

Draw out worries, concerns etc

Use **PCC example** to demonstrate need for personal statement

Explain Job Description and Person Spec

11.45am Personal Statement exercise

In pairs, look at person spec and Job description. Discuss what you would write to address each criterion.

Take feedback.

Show **Tom's example.**

12.05am Jobsearch

Input – importance of being proactive, networking, attitude etc

Where and how to look

Writing a spec letter – where to find who to send spec letters to.

Any Q's?

Evaluation

12.30 Close

Resources needed:

Laptop/Projector for PowerPoint
Flipchart/pens
CV Handouts
Example CV's
Example application forms
Personal Statement example

COURSE TITLE It's Never Too Late to Change Career

SESSION No.1 of 3 TOPIC: What else could you do?

OBJECTIVE(S):- By the end of the session students will:
have listed some ideas for jobs that would suit them, & begun to form goals and an action plan; feel better, more hopeful.

Time	Activities / Content	Teaching Method	Equipment and Materials
9.30	Tea/Coffee and Introductions Objectives	Tutor led discussion Pair discussion Feed back to group	Flip Chart & pens Name cards Client1 forms OHP & OHT Egan's 3 stages
10.00	Where are you now – How do you feel?	Pair discussion (other side)	
10.20	Where do you want to be – free thought.	Listen to CD and doodle on blank page	CD player + CD Booklets-p4 Pencils/crayons
10.30	What do you want from your work?	Work alone Values card sort	Values cards Booklets p5-7
11.00	**BREAK**	**BREAK**	**BREAK**
11.15	Where are you now – What can you do?	In pairs with someone of similar background.	Workbooks.
11.35	Where do you want to be? Interests.	Complete Interests Questionnaire Tutor explanation	Biros and highlighter pens Questionnaires
12.00	Where do you want to be? Set Goals.	Explain about goals, and 1:1	Flip Chart & pens Biros
12.15	How will you get there? Write Action Plan.	Work alone with tutor support.	Action Plan forms SMART OHT
12.30	Evaluation and Plan next steps	Alone	Evaluation forms Diaries
12.45	**CLOSE**	**CLOSE**	**CLOSE**

Winning Respect and Recognition Programme

Outcomes:
To equip staff to identify factors that affect their reputation
To identify ways of improving professionalism and confidence

12.30 pm Negative reversal exercise how to make sure we are never respected and/or recognised!

12.45 First impressions **OHT PMI scan** (plus, minus, interesting)
OHT Why people get promoted

1.05pm Join the CIA (Confidence, Integrity, Amiability)
Pairs - How do you know if someone is confident? What are the ingredients/attributes?
What would it take for you to be able to model your behaviour on theirs? (gap analysis)
(NB Behaviour is all people can see)

1.20pm Integrity
Exercise **Handout p6** What damages our integrity
Small groups. Think about self and what they see in others

1.40pm Amiability
Look at **Maslow model p8**
Different small groups – APC-exercise (alternatives, possibilities, choices)
What can we do in the work place to meet the needs of others as defined by Maslow?
What happens if you have CI without A? CA without I? AI without C? (3 groups taking one each)

1.50pm What will you do differently?

2pm Close

Assertiveness Programme

Outcomes:

- To be able to define what being assertive means
- To recognise own behavioural style
- To state two action points to improve assertiveness

12.30pm Define assertiveness

When is it difficult to be assertive? – list on flipchart

Group discussion What are the obstacles to assertiveness? (Lack of awareness, anxiety, negative self-talk, verbal deficit, behavioural deficit) Can we classify them in any way? (internal/external)
How can we deal with them? (Pay attention to any that are not covered by the rest of the programme)

Brainstorm benefits of being assertive
Handout Benefits of being assertive

12.50pm Handout Rights and Responsibilities p 3
What is the initial reaction to this?
Do they agree with statement about the neglect of responsibilities?
Ask them to look at it for five minutes, and personalise it to suit themselves e.g. star things they feel strongly about, question mark by the things they are not sure about, delete anything not relevant.
Is there anything they would add?

1.05pm Handouts Evaluate Your Behaviour p 1
Talk through, ensuring group understand the four types.
Exercise (15 mins) in pairs or small groups, list the following:
Aggressive..............................Passive
Manipulative...........................Assertive
What are the advantages and disadvantages of each one?
When are they appropriate or inappropriate?
Where do you see each one?
What would happen if you take each non assertive behaviour to extreme?

cont'd next page...

cont'd from previous page

1.20pm Handout Assertive Interaction
Work through, check understanding
Discussion – How different is this from our usual practice?
What is the hardest thing? What are you already pretty good at?

1.30pm Exercise In pairs (10 mins), refer back to the difficult situations we listed earlier. Discuss what behaviour are you using in these situations currently? Why do you think this is?
Choose one each to role play using 3 stage model.

Feedback to group
What part was most difficult?
Are there any parts that you feel you already do well?

1.45pm Handout Techniques (4 pages)

Run through the rest of the techniques handout, drawing attention to things that have not already been drawn out.

1.50pm Handout Listen and Learn

Work through. You can read hundreds of books on assertiveness, but you will not change unless you practice!

Ask the group to reflect on the session, look back over the handouts, and mark areas that they feel are relevant to them.

Ask them to choose two things that they will begin to work on.

We hope that these plans (in our own personal shorthand) made sense and that you have started to get some ideas for your group session. Perhaps you have already started to plan it.

Have you noticed how we have been taking you through Kolb's learning cycle? Part One reflected on the skills you already have and how you can apply them to working with groups. Part Two provided some theory and Part Three has been about planning to put theory into practice. Now all that remains is to take the plunge, and do it.

Part Four moves you into the session. It looks at things that might happen in the room and how to manage them to get the best out of every situation.

Part Four
Managing the Group

Often how to manage the group is a bigger worry than what to include in the programme. To a large extent we can control the resources we prepare, our knowledge, and how organised we are. How the group will respond to us, and to each other, can be a big unknown – and with the unknown, the fear factor often arrives.

People do behave differently in groups. You can have a friendly, rational conversation one to one with a school student, only to find when you run a group session with his class that he fools around and does whatever it takes to get a laugh from his mates. Attitudes and atmospheres are infectious and individuals will quickly adapt to the norm that they find in the group – a gloomy, unmotivated person can pick up the group's hope and enthusiasm ... or the reverse can happen.

This section is here to help you discover techniques for managing the behaviour of the group. We will look at specific common behaviours that you may encounter, give you strategies to help you manage tricky situations and look at making group dynamics work to your advantage.

What can you do when...........

- People are so enthusiastic that timing has gone to the wind?
- The group are passive, unresponsive - everything seems flat?
- People are feeding off each other's whinges?
- They are more interested in each other than the task in hand?
- You feel you've completely lost control?

As a group leader, you need to be pretty much unflappable and prepared to cope with whatever situation arises. Arm yourself with the tools that follow, but you'd better resign yourself now to the fact that human behaviour is incredibly complex, varies hugely and is never entirely predictable!

Dealing with the Group

Rule No 1 and Rule No 2

There is one thing you can be sure of - if the group detect you are uncomfortable, apprehensive or anxious, in no time at all they will have picked up your mood and they will be out of sorts too. Have you ever been to a presentation or lesson where the person at the front was nervous, stammering or pouring with sweat, or where the speaker is unprepared or pitches the material at the wrong level for the group? It's painful, isn't it? It's hardly conducive to learning, or participation, so always remember Rule No 1.

Rule No 1 is absolutely critical for success in groupwork. You may muddle through without it, but you would be on very risky ground. The good news is that Rule No 1 is incredibly simple to learn. It's not always quite so easy to put into practice, but if you have developed one to one skill, you're half way there - you just need to adapt it to the group setting. So what is it, this all important mantra?

It is merely this:

Rule No 1

Behave as if you expect a successful, enjoyable session.

It may be simple, but it carries with it substantial wisdom. Think about what it means, and how it unfolds to your group. To a large degree, you can equate it to the Bedford steps we looked at in Part One –

Creating a friendly, welcoming atmosphere, and contracting about what will occur.

Let's unpick it a bit.

"Behave as if..."

You may well have come across variations on this theme, taught in all sorts of courses, such as confidence building, assertiveness, interview techniques or presentation skills, where phrases like *"behave to become"* or *"act it to be it"* are used to convey the message that if you work at making your body language, speech, manner and smile portray how you want to feel, eventually your emotions and mind will catch up and you will feel more confident and less anxious.

It may feel impossible to act "not nervous" when you're scared witless, but it can be achieved. Besides a strong determination, the other factor that is crucial is that you have a very clear understanding and feeling of what it is you want to achieve. Visualisation techniques can help here (we discuss these briefly in The One to One Toolkit). Spend time imagining how you will come across to your group. What will you be wearing? How will you be standing? What will your speech sound like? What will your body language be like? How will they be responding to you? Keep on until not only do you have a crystal clear picture of the New Improved You, but also you can recall it so well, it is becoming part of you already.

"...you expect a successful..."

So you're learning how to portray a confident image - but in what context? You also need a very clear idea of what success will look like. It will be made up of several factors that you need to explore, some relating to the process – what happens during the session – and some to the outcomes – what your group members will have achieved by the end. Let's look at these in turn:

Process

You can visualise a successful process during the session, for example, your input and exercises being well received and productive, participants being engaged throughout.

Outcomes

You can also fast forward in your mind to the end of the session. You have achieved what you set out to do. The participants are now confident and equipped for interviews. They have produced a new CV. They have learned something useful and they are cheerful and positive, thanking you for your help.

A vital part of your preparation is to find a quiet moment beforehand to think through what success will **feel** like, **look** like and **sound** like. Visualising this in advance and fixing it in your mind will help you with Rule No 1.

"...enjoyable session"

Enjoyment isn't just about lightweight froth without meaning. There are lots of elements to a groupwork session that your participants may enjoy, such as:

- A challenge
- The opportunity to experience something new
- Meeting new people
- Getting to know others better and forging friendships
- A sense of achievement
- The chance to speak out and be heard
- Shared stories and experiences
- Getting fears and concerns out into the open
- Feeling motivated by getting the tools to do something
- A sense of belonging

...and we haven't even mentioned learning yet!

Often, what people enjoy most in a session is not something we planned for. We organise the programme and the resources and then somehow the team spirit kicks in – the group bond and share.

How many of this list do you expect to occur in your session? Can you think of other factors that could be added?

There are very few types of groupwork where none of the above will apply. If you act as if the session will be enjoyable, you are giving your group permission to relax and get the very best from it.

Rule No 2

What is your worst nightmare? Losing control? Things going badly wrong? People getting angry or walking out? Being laughed at?

These are all quite extreme situations, and they really don't happen very often. They are unlikely to happen at all if you follow:

Rule No 2

Head them off at the pass

To effectively head them off at the pass, you need to know which way they are going. Rule no 2 is about being alert at all times (one reason why running a group is so tiring!) so you will spot the warning signs that trouble is brewing. When you see a sign, you nip the potential problem in the bud. It may be that the situation or behaviour would never have escalated into trouble, but you're not going to give it the chance to find out.

This means that it isn't an extra coffee break for you if the group has been put in pairs or small groups to complete a task. You should always be paying attention, listening in or walking round to check that they are on task and not struggling. Normally just your presence will remind them of the job in hand. What are the tell-tale signs to look out for? They may include:

- Restlessness, such as drumming fingers, fidgeting, texting under the table
- Not attending to the task in hand
- Personal conversations going on, members distracting each other
- Tuning out, day dreaming
- Hostile expression or body language

Ideally, you will always have a few tricks up your sleeve to distract or divert attention, such as:

- A spare exercise that requires them to work differently, eg: if they are wandering off topic while working in pairs, bring them back to work as a whole group
- A new visual aid or different form of media that will grab attention, eg: a DVD
- A story to illustrate a point
- A quick fire quiz

Anything, in fact, that changes the situation. Introducing changes will not mean that you lose the focus of the session, since all your optional extras will be related to the task in hand; it just means that you are prepared for any eventuality. By making the group face something new, you will keep them on their toes.

It may be that you become concerned about an individual, or you want to talk to some of the group about their behaviour. Often this is best addressed by dealing discreetly with the people concerned, rather than bringing it up in front of the whole group. You have a couple of options here. You could have an unscheduled extra tea break, or just announce that everyone should “take five” to stretch legs or get some fresh air, giving you a chance to pin down those you want to talk to. Alternatively, you could choose an exercise that splits the group up, so that you can talk to some while the rest are getting on with a task.

Side Conversations

Side conversations are a common bugbear of groupwork. You are trying to explain a topic, only to find that a couple of participants are carrying on their own private conversation. It is hard to tell if their chatter is related to the subject in hand or not. Either way, it distracts other group members and you.

Usually, moving casually towards them while you are talking and trying to make eye contact will do the trick. If that fails, you can try to draw them into the main discussion by asking their opinion or if they would like to share their thoughts with the whole group. A good humoured *"Please can we have one conversation at a time?"* is direct and to the point. As a last resort you can stop what you are doing and wait for them to notice.

There is a danger here that you might fall into the trap of treating them like naughty children. If we are working with adults, it is important that we respond to them accordingly.

Shifting Your Attention

One of the key skills of groupwork, that you will not have needed in one to one advising, is shifting your attention. You will need to learn to switch back and forth regularly throughout the session between scanning the whole group and focusing on individuals. You are likely to do this naturally to a large degree, but it is worth monitoring yourself to make sure that you are getting the balance right.

If you have been working as an adviser, it may come more naturally to you to try to concentrate on each person's needs. For example, if you have given a task to individuals or small groups, it's easy to get drawn to one person or group who ask for your help, and not notice what's happening in the rest of the room. A successful group leader will respond to individuals, but not to the detriment of the group by giving too much attention to one person. Be aware, people can get annoyed if they think you are not sharing your attention equally – it suggests you have favourites and are ignoring the others.

On the other hand, if you're used to giving presentations to large groups of people, you are more likely to be aware of the overview of what is going on in the room. The other extreme is that you are so busy organising activities and showing PowerPoint, that individual group members may be disengaged or have concerns, and they get overlooked.

There is no strict guideline to adhere to – just be aware that if you have been in one mode for a while, step back and check the other before continuing.

How are groups different?

The short answer is that every group is different! They may have common threads, but each one is unique, which is one of the many reasons why groupwork is so rewarding; there is always a new experience and something for you to learn and reflect on. Even so, some thought about the different types of group will be useful, because it can alter how you prepare.

Below is a list of some ways in which groups differ. Think through each one. How would knowing where your group fits change your approach? What differences would you make to your programme to appeal to each type?

Formal	>	Informal
New	>	Established
Voluntary attendance	>	Mandatory attendance
Large numbers	>	Small numbers
Clear expectations	>	Unrealistic expectations
Highly qualified	>	Foundation level
Good health	>	Long term health problems
Defined age group	>	Mixed ages

Let's have a quick look at each of these to help define the terms. We can't do justice to them fully here – some of them would take a book by themselves to explore – but hopefully we can give some pointers for handling them and some food for thought.

Of course, it's highly probable that your group will fall into several of these categories, so you will need to take account of all of the types that are relevant to you.

Formal > Informal

A formal group will usually be part of an existing institution, such as a college, training provider or even a club or community association such as the WI. Participants will have been through a joining or enrolling process, which in some cases may have been selective. They may be working towards a qualification or gaining life skills.

The important thing to remember here is that a formal group may have set ways of doing things – for example record keeping, procedures, house rules or etiquette – that you need to find out about in advance. You might want to find out what else, if anything, the group have done on your topic. It will help you choose appropriate activities if you have good understanding of the context the group are functioning in.

An informal group may have little more in common than turning up in the same place at the same time, although usually there is some common interest. Examples would be: people who have responded to a poster or advertisement inviting them to come along and find out about a topic; self managed groups of friends who have taken it upon themselves to support each other through things like study or job hunting; drop in sessions where you find you have six people wanting help at the same time; a group of mums at a pre-school centre.

In these cases, you have more freedom to choose how to run the group, but you might have to do more thinking on your feet and be flexible in your approach. Some informal groups might actually respond badly to activities that are too planned or formal – anything that hints of school – so you may need to appear very casual, and appear to be just chatting and try to introduce your topic gently into the conversation. Try to pick up on their interests and link your topic to these, although you will have prepared in your mind and brought materials for a whole range of activities you could do, if they seem ready.

New > Established

This one is fairly self explanatory. On the one hand you have people who have not met before, on the other you have folk who are already working together and know each other well. They will have fallen into patterns of behaviour, such as who sits where or who speaks on behalf of the others. One obvious advantage with an established group is that you do not need to spend time breaking the ice and getting them to know each other. Asking them to introduce themselves to you is a much shorter task, and will give you a feel for how they relate to each other.

It is still important for both new and established groups that you clarify the contract, e.g. how you will be working together, what you can and can't do for them. Established groups may well make assumptions about you based on their experience unless you tell them otherwise. If they often meet for learning sessions, they may have expectations about the methods you will use. They may be resistant to new ideas, such as breaking into small groups, or of course they may welcome them. They may expect you to be completely competent in using their technology for exciting multi-media presentations and see your flip chart as very old fashioned.

New groups may not know what to expect. You will need to put more effort into helping them relax with you and each other. Ideas for icebreakers are in Part Three.

Voluntary attendance > Mandatory attendance

It is hardly surprising that those who attend a group session through choice often do so with more enthusiasm than those who are forced to attend. This does not mean that mandatory sessions are always difficult, because they are not, but you do need to be aware that group members have not necessarily bought into the process. On the positive side, your session may be viewed as an interesting alternative to their usual activities.

Mandatory sessions usually arise as a result of the individual being under some obligation to an organisation that has power over them, and can sanction them if they fail to attend. Examples include the Probation Service or the Job Centre sending them, or when you are asked to do a lesson in a school or college, giving you a captive audience. It usually helps to get this out into the open, asking what brings them here today. If you get the answer "we were sent", you have a starting point from which to work and find a way to win their interest and co-operation.

Large numbers > Small numbers

What we mean by large and small numbers will vary, partly due to our usual working practice. We would see a small group consisting of between about four and twelve people. With fewer than four, there will not be enough variety or balance, and you may find yourself dealing with each individual separately even though they are in the same room. Groups of six or twelve are especially useful, giving you the option of work in pairs, threes or small groups yet still small enough for a whole group discussion. You can keep your manner fairly gentle and personal.

When a group gets much larger than 15, you might have to spend more time presenting to the whole group and giving them tasks to work on individually. You will probably have a larger room and therefore need to pay special attention to your presence and making sure you can be heard. PowerPoint will be of more use than a flip chart if the room is large and people are far away from you.

Large groups may appear to offer less chance for interaction between members, but you can still get a large group to do interactive work. For example if they are seated café style round tables of six or eight, tasks can be given and each table choose a spokesperson to report back. Even if they are sitting in rows, lecture theatre style, you can hand out sheets (eg: quizzes) for them to do in pairs, or you can ask them to discuss a question with the person next to them, to start them thinking about it before you present to the whole group. You usually find a few of your audience who are not afraid to feed back in front of a large group, though you will have to manage their input to keep it brief.

Clear expectations > Unrealistic expectations

Sometimes people have a clear idea what to expect from a session, while at other times they have acquired a picture that is wide of the mark. It can save you considerable time and difficulty if you can to find out in advance what they expect. If you have not been responsible for the promotion of the session, or have not seen the joining instructions that were sent out, make it your business to see a copy of any email or letter the participants have received.

If the session has been organised by a colleague, particularly if they work for another organisation, have a chat with them and ask them what they have said about the session. It is not uncommon for colleagues working elsewhere to have a hazy notion of what your organisation actually does. Doing this little piece of groundwork will help you manage the group's expectations, and can also help you avoid being introduced in a way that puts undue pressure on you – *"This is Susan – she's an expert, she'll know which university course is best for every one of you!"*

Highly qualified > Foundation level

Many years ago, we worked together running an executive jobsearch programme. Participants were typically quite highly qualified middle managers facing redundancy. They were articulate, could cope with lengthy periods of concentration, and had the techniques and experience to problem solve and evaluate options effectively.

The other side of the coin are those groups that training providers call pre-entry. They may have learning difficulties, behavioural problems that impeded their learning at school, or perhaps just didn't attend school very often. Just sitting still and concentrating on a task may be very challenging for them.

For maximum effectiveness you will need to make sure that your approach, as well as the content, format and style of your materials, will suit the needs of the group. You will also need to think about the type of activities you organise and the length of the session, based on their attention span. Remember not to make assumptions, though. A highly effective senior manager might have some form of dyslexia and gain little from activities too strongly based on the written word, while those pre-entry behaviour problems could stem from boredom with tasks that are too simple rather than from a learning difficulty.

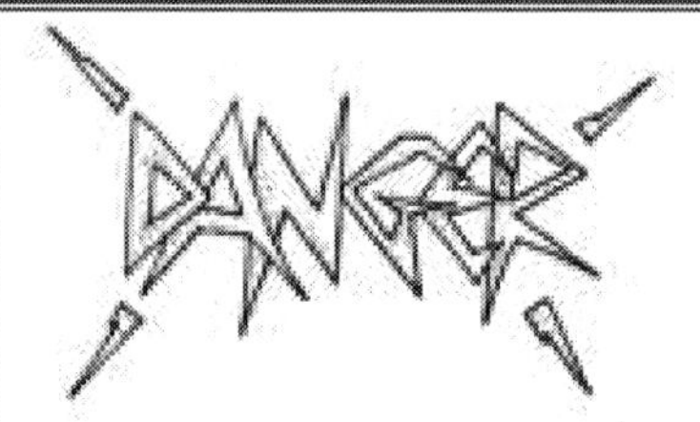

CHECK THE LEVEL!

Julie was asked to do a workshop for staff facing redundancy, and was given materials to use that were appropriate for staff with a high standard of literacy.

The company then sent along several lads who had been employed on the production line. They were skilled people, but were out of practice at working with words. They found the materials intimidating and difficult to work with.

Fortunately all was not lost on this occasion, as she had thrown a few extras into her bag, such as simpler handouts and card sorts that suited them much better. Never assume that the tools you have been provided with are right for the job!

Good health > Long term health problems

People recovering from health problems or learning to manage with permanent conditions can often benefit from working in groups. With any group, it is always worth checking if anyone has a health issue that might affect them during the session and if so, how. This is often asked before the day – some trainers make a point of phoning each participant in advance to introduce themselves and find out any concerns they may have.

You can then think about how to adapt your activities. Examples of adaptations might include more frequent coffee breaks, as concentration can be an issue with some forms of medication. Frequent breaks also give folk a chance to walk around, as sitting in one place can be problematic for those with back problems. Back sufferers may prefer to stand or walk about, or even lie on the floor! You can adapt handouts for those with poor eyesight, and if anyone has bad repetitive strain injury or arthritis in hands and wrists, reduce the amount of writing or ask if they want someone else to write for them.

Most people with health conditions know how to manage them, so as long as you ask, there is usually a way to still achieve your goals. It is always best to ask the individual what would help them to get the most from the session, rather than make assumptions about what people with a particular condition are likely to need.

Defined age group > Mixed ages

People often tend to relate better to others who are near their own age, so sometimes it can take a little longer for a group to gel if you have a wide age group. This need not be a problem – once they have got to know each other, people of different ages can be supportive to each other and benefit from the broad range of experience in the room.

Do bear age in mind when choosing the materials to use. You may wish to adapt them to make them 'youth friendly' if you have a group of younger people and check that materials are not too childish for adults. Also be aware of dates – you may have a good anecdote from 1982, but your group will find it hard to relate to it if they weren't born!

These are just some examples of how groups can differ. You can probably think of many more, such as same or mixed gender, motivated or de-motivated, similar or different backgrounds, etc. The best advice will always be to find out as much as you can about your group in advance, so that you can think through the implications for your preparation, facilitation style and materials. If in doubt, be prepared to learn from your group. If you go in with an open mind, consult them and listen to what they tell you, you will learn what motivates and concerns people from a diverse range of backgrounds and develop your ability to deliver successful group sessions in every situation.

Dealing with Individuals

How do you deal with.....

- Ramona the Rambler?
- Norbert the Negative?
- Sylvester the Silent?
- Horace the Hostile?
- Nora the Know it All?
- Velda the Victim?

Ramona the Rambler

The Rambler is the person who thinks out loud and enjoys conversation. Unfortunately she tends to lose focus – her comments go off subject and wander all over the place.

A little rambling now and again is no bad thing. It can help build rapport or bring a bit of light relief. But there comes a point when you need to rein Ramona in, before so much time disappears that you may not achieve the session's goals.

You could try:

- Moving, to act as a cue that something different is about to happen. For example, if you are sitting, stand up and move to the flipchart. If you are already standing, you could move to your desk and pick up your notes.

- Using subtle body language cues, like raising your hand or glancing at the clock (you'll probably find yourself doing this subconsciously). Nodding three times is also quite effective to indicate that it is time to move on.

- Inviting Ramona, and anyone else who is interested in her ramble, to continue chatting about it over coffee.
- Saying that if there is time left at the end of the session, we can hear more about Ramona's story.
- Thanking Ramona for contributing, and asking if you can return to the main topic. It is important to be good humoured as far as possible. The Ramona's we encounter are often those who have found confidence and a voice by being part of the group, and are acting out of enthusiasm. It would be sad if they were to feel reprimanded for getting a little carried away.
- Following the above moves with some direct questions to the whole group about the topic in hand, to get back on task.

Norbert the Negative

As in the workplace, Norbert can be one of the most destructive people. We've discussed previously how groups can be synergistic, motivating and inspiring through the energy created. Unfortunately, the opposite is also true; negativity can very quickly spread through the group, particularly when it is vocalised persistently. Occasionally, other group members will challenge Norbert. This can make for an interesting session and save you having to do it yourself, but it can get out of hand unless you contain it.

Negativity can be the offspring of frustration, habit, or inability to think differently about a situation. We can get trapped into deep ruts, making it hard to change our perception. The good news is that the buzz of a group can be an effective tool for seeing things in a new way.

You could try:

- Revisiting your ground rules. Have you included anything about being constructive? If referring back to your ground rules isn't going to add sufficient weight, you may need to rephrase them or introduce a new one that gives firmer boundaries. You can see example ground rules in Part Three.

- Having a Parking Area. This means having a whiteboard or flipchart where you can record ('park') issues arising that are outside the parameters of the session, such as not being able to change the policy of other organisations. You can agree with your group what will be done with the results.

- Helping the group to differentiate between what they can change and what they can't, and then helping them to understand that their energy is much better expended where it can have some effect, as opposed to banging one's head against the proverbial brick wall.

- Asking the group to work on each other's problems. It can be much easier to see the wood from the trees for someone else's situation. They could work in pairs, threes, or – if the group is not too large – take a look at one issue from each person in turn.

- Using a framework such as De Bono's Six Hats (we described these in The One to One Toolkit). Each hat is a different colour, representing a different way of viewing a situation. They help people look at the other side of the coin: *"So, that's the negative side of the situation, Norbert. Now put on the yellow hat. Can you see any positives that could arise?"*. If Norbert can't see any, maybe the rest of the group can.

- Using positive reinforcement. Look for constructive or helpful aspects of the situation, and note them, sharing them with others where appropriate. Bring them to the attention of your group when pessimism creeps in. Reward only positive behaviour – do this by just saying thank you, being encouraging or giving a small treat. When others behave in a positive way, draw attention to it. Ignore negative behaviour – do not reward it by arguing with it or criticising, as this attention will encourage the offender to repeat the behaviour.

- Focusing on the future and what he wants, rather than the past and what he did not like. You may need to spend some time helping Norbert to work out what the preferred situation is, but once he can describe or visualise a positive outcome, it will be easier to encourage him to work towards it.

- Being assertive. You do not have to listen to others complaining all the time, particularly if you have already heard the issues several times. Start by letting Norbert know that you have heard his complaints and you understand how he feels (if you do). You are within your rights to ask people to stop being negative and to tell them of the impact it has on you and others. Remain pleasant, but stand your ground.

- Agreeing with him. You may not like how Norbert expresses himself, but he may have a point. Knowing that he has been heard and hearing his point validated may free him to begin to change his attitude.

- Combining agreeing with him with also pointing out time restraints (particularly if he is being repetitive). Offering to discuss the problem with him privately.

Changing Colin

Colin was a major moaner, everyone knew it. He complained about the changes in his company, how they had been implemented, how they had made his job harder and lowered morale everywhere.

He came on a workshop to look at the impact of change. While learning about the Change Curve, which explains people's different reactions to change, the penny dropped for Colin. He realised that he had a choice, that other ways to behave were available. He decided to try another way.

His Boss reported that he became a different, more positive, person overnight.

Sylvester the Silent

Sylvester may not appear to disrupt the group like Ramona or Norbert does, but the atmosphere can be noticeable when it is obvious to others that one person is not participating. Sometimes it is not an issue at all - Sylvester may just be a reflective learner, whose preference is to absorb what is going on around him, and needs time to process what he has heard. He may not like working in groups; he may be shy, under-confident or just unsure of what to say. Some sensitivity is required here; to push him too far out of his comfort zone could alienate him completely. On the other hand, his silence could make the rest of the group uncomfortable so, as always, you have a balancing act to achieve.

You could try:

- Giving the group a task or worksheet to complete individually. You will then at least out find whether it is the group or the topic that is causing his silence.

- Asking the group to work in pairs. Sylvester will only have to talk to one person, which he may find easier, and he will find it much harder to remain silent. You can then move round the room and check on all the pairs, which gives you the opportunity to talk to Sylvester while there is background conversation going on. Hopefully you will be able to find out if he is OK, and why he is saying so little.

- If you have been able to talk to Sylvester in his pair, you may be able to mention something he said when taking group feedback. This is effective in more than one way. Firstly, if Sylvester is struggling with shyness or lack of confidence, he may feel more part of the group if he has heard his opinion or comments valued. Secondly, other group members may relax more if they have heard a contribution from Sylvester, albeit indirectly.

- Addressing questions individually to all group members, including Sylvester. Do this with a light touch: you are trying to encourage, not embarrass him. If he cannot or will not respond, spare his blushes and move on in good humour, saying something like *"Maybe you need a minute to think about that….."*

- Weaving in an introduction to learning styles. You could describe the styles briefly to the group (see Part Two) to make the point that we are all different, so it is normal for a group to display a range of behaviours. This may make the group relax a little and stop worrying about Sylvester. Anyway, wouldn't it be boring if we were all the same?

Horace the Hostile

Often you will spot Horace's attitude by his body language, before he has spoken a word. His arms are often folded, appearing to put a barrier between you and him, his brow is often furrowed, or his face set in a humourless fashion when the rest of the group are smiling and relaxed. He often chooses to sit as far away from you as he can manage, with his back to you or partially so. Whereas Norbert the Negative may display a victim 'poor old me' mentality, Horace is much more open and upfront with his hostility.

Horace will have a reason for his hostility, even if he does not recognise it himself. He may be angry that he has been 'made' to come along, making him feel powerless. He might think that he does not need the session – who are you to tell him what to do? He may have had a bad experience of another group, and is squaring up as experience points to this group being just as unhelpful. Alternatively, he may be painfully aware that he does need some help and be scared that he won't understand and may be belittled or unable to cope. His hostility may manifest itself in cynicism, a "them and us" approach, or just sheer frustration aimed at anyone in his path.

As you have the whole group to deal with, it is possible that you won't be able to give him the individual attention required to get to the bottom of his hostility – but you will need to handle the situation to stop it having a negative impact on the others in the group. You will need to make a judgement call on whether or not you are going to try and find out the reason for his hostility. You will find it easier to deal with a known problem than an unknown issue, but there is a danger that the whole session could be taken up with discussing the issue. On the other hand, if you follow our Rule Number One (see the start of Part Four), Horace may well soften and change his attitude once he sees your friendly professionalism, and discovers that his fears will not materialise. Often the wisest option is to wait a while, give Horace the chance to settle, and then re-evaluate the situation.

Do be aware of your own body language when dealing with Horace. It is very easy to tense your shoulders or look worried when faced with hostility, but this will look like defensiveness and could well exacerbate the situation. Self awareness is critical here, so do check yourself and make sure that you behave in a consistent manner towards all your group members. A calm, confident, tolerant manner, standing tall and squarely, with a firm gaze, slow smooth movements and a slight smile should show you care about and value Horace but you are not afraid of him and you intend to deliver the group's objectives.

So, what can we do to limit, or hopefully eliminate completely, the damage that Horace could wreak on your session? Some of the tips above for dealing with Norbert are relevant. Here are some more:

- Remember that the hostility or aggression may be masking fear. How would you approach a fearful person? Respond to the fear, not the hostility. We know we keep going on about contracting the ground rules and boundaries, but they can really deal with Horace's fear by telling him who you are, what role he is expected to play, and why you are all there.

- If you get an aggressive response to a question, ask the same question to more positive or supportive group members. It may be beneficial for Horace to see that there are other ways to respond.

- It is OK to disagree. You don't want to spend the whole session arguing, so agree to differ in a good humoured way and move on.

- You may also be able to build on what Horace has said, linking it back to the topic, or using it as an anecdote to make a point. If you can do this, Horace's views or voice will have been acknowledged. Never underestimate the power or importance of having your voice heard. Horace may well find his anger deflating as he recognises that you have valued his contribution.

- We said earlier that Horace often chooses to put as much distance as he can between himself and the group leader. Moving towards him and maintaining eye contact can change the dynamic.

- Always allow Horace a way to gracefully retreat from a confrontation. It can be difficult to change behaviour, especially if it is entrenched or laden with high emotion. Make it easy for him to back down.

- Talk to Horace privately during a break. Try to find out what makes him tick and choose something to chat about that interests you both.

- Everyone is allowed to have feelings. You could bring it the open by saying: "You seem really angry about this. Does anyone else feel this way?"

- Ignore the behaviour. If you are short of time, and have important content to convey, this can be the best option. How will the other group members feel if you spend so long trying to pacify Horace that they leave without what they came for?

- Sometimes a good humoured trade-off works. For example, "So, if I promise to put you in contact with someone who will help you with your benefit problems straight after this session, will you stop complaining about other organisations?"

- As a last resort, you could privately ask the individual to leave for the good of the group. Some people think that you are paid to be there and they assume that you have to put up with bad behaviour limitlessly. Hopefully you won't, as it is just not fair on the rest of the group, nor on you. You should always know how the organisation you are working with deals with the eventuality of someone being asked to leave the session.

- If Horace is not just Hostile but plain Horrible to either you or to one or more other members of the group, then you will definitely need to take clear action. You need to keep everyone safe and also be seen by the group not to tolerate aggressive, bullying or discriminatory behaviour. Refer back to the ground rules you contracted at the start, state them more clearly, describe the behaviour that is breaking the rules and give Horace an ultimatum. So that you can stick to this, again, make sure you know in advance what the rules are and what help you can call on to protect yourself and other group members.

Several Horaces at once

Julie: I once had a friendly group who were working well together. They were adults with long term health problems, so had been out of the job market for a long time. Confidence levels were low, and literacy was shaky for many of them.

One week I mentioned that we would be looking at Jobsearch. All of a sudden, Horace became the alter ego of half of the group. They became grumpy, muttering that it would be a waste of time. Arms were folded, eyes fixed firmly on the floor.

I asked them what they expected the session to be like. It turned out that they had all previously been 'sent' to a local training provider to learn about Jobsearch. They had been put in a room with a pile of newspapers, and told to get on with it, without any instruction, encouragement or assistance to help them address their barriers.

They found the experience a real confidence killer. Imagine being asked to phone an employer, when you don't know what to say, and a group of people are listening? Or being told to fill in an application form, when you don't know what you should be writing?

Fortunately, having brought their expectations and experience out into the open, I was able to assure them that this session would be different. The Horaces were doubting at first, and nervous about proceeding, but they soon found out that all sessions with the title Jobsearch cannot be tarred with the same brush. The secret was to tell them I'd noticed they weren't happy, and to ask them why. Once you know what's wrong, it can be very easy to put it right, and you've shown you care how they feel.

Nora the Know It All

Nora may be related to Ramona the rambler, inasmuch as they both like the sound of their own voice and may be in fine spirits. It can just be enthusiasm; how good do we feel when we are asked about a topic we know something about? We can all be proud to share our knowledge and experience. Often there are too few opportunities to show what we know, so the group session may well have the novelty factor.

Other Nora's are a little more insidious and their motives, which may be subconscious, are more about the need for attention or power. Their method for feeling good, which may be masking an underlying lack of self esteem, is to put others down or show their superiority. Here, you are balancing the tightrope between helping Nora to feel good by validating her contribution (providing she has got it right – another problem comes when the know-it-all starts giving out wrong information), and treating the rest of the group fairly by not letting her dominate or take up time that should be given to others.

Do bear in mind that that everyone in your group is likely to know more than you do about lots things. You are leading the group because you have something to offer, but never fall into the trap of thinking you know it all. One of the greatest joys of running a group is discovering all their talents, knowledge and experiences so that the group has a fresh new pool to draw from and share. Rejoice in it. If you try to be the oracle of all wisdom, you are making a rod for your own back, and limiting the potential of the group.

Several of the tips for dealing with Ramona will also apply to Nora. Here are some others to consider:

- When asking for comment, make it clear that you are looking for a short reply, not a speech. Using phrases like *"Can you tell me, in a nutshell......"* or *"Give me one sentence that sums up......."* *"Describe your views in three words...."*

- Thank her for her contribution. Emphasise the parts that are most relevant, maybe summarising them.

- If she really does know more than most, and this is obvious to all, there is nothing wrong in asking her to hold back until everyone else has thought about the subject in hand, or going round the group and coming to her last. This gives the others a chance, but also will help her feel valued, as it is recognition of her knowledge.

- Give Nora individual attention during breaks. If she gets the chance to show what she knows and get it off her chest, Nora may well be more contented and less forceful when the group reconvenes.

Velda the Victim

Velda is possibly the most frustrating of all group members. Velda is the participant who behaves like an underdog. She has no control over her life because she lets everyone else take charge. If things go wrong, no responsibility lies with her. She is resigned to her lot.

She quite likes sitting next to Norbert the Negative because he understands her the most. She nods sympathetically when he is moaning. The difference between them is that Norbert can vocalise the negative side of anything, misdirecting his personal power, whereas Velda is quieter, caught up in her own 'Poor old me' world, and feels completely powerless.

You could view Velda as the antithesis of learning. All the good outcomes we seek to achieve, like increasing participants' confidence, enabling them to learn new skills and equipping them to move forward, can be water off a duck's back to Velda. Good things happen to other people, not her. "There's no point," "What can you do?" are phrases you'll often hear. Please resist the temptation to pick her up and shake her! She may be the biggest challenge, but she also is capable of showing the most change and progressing more than most.

How can we help Velda take some responsibility for herself? Her thinking habits are often deeply ingrained, so progress can be slow. If you get the opportunity to work with Velda over several weeks, you may well be surprised at how she responds to encouragement.

- Break tasks down as far as possible, so that you can help Velda to see the progress she has made with each small step.

- Every small step counts, as Velda is not in the habit of recognising when she has done well. Point out her successes. Even turning up can be an achievement for some. Always find something to praise her for, but make sure you can back it up with evidence, because she will notice empty flattery.

- Use the group to affirm Velda's worth. Even new groups will often support each other and challenge lack of self esteem when they notice it. Going round the room asking everyone to say one thing they admire about each other person is one way of doing it.

- Ask the others if any of them have faced similar difficulties to Velda. Examples and stories from her peers are likely to have more impact then those from you.

Tiredness, Tears and Tantrums

Just a few more of the behaviours that we have coped with during our time as groupwork facilitators, these are probably examples of some of our cast of characters taken to the extreme. What should you do if the Sylvester the Silent actually turns out to be asleep, or even if he just keeps yawning? How should you handle it if Horace's hostility or Norbert's negativity build up to an angry outburst either at the state of the world, at your incompetence or at the opinions expressed by another group member? What about when Velda feels so bad about her situation or Nora's veneer of confidence cracks, and they burst into floods of tears?

The reinforcement technique of ignoring unwanted behaviour is inappropriate here for several reasons. First, none of these responses will be intentional or pre-meditated and the individuals are likely to be surprised and ashamed at showing themselves up in front of the group. The rest of the group will be either embarrassed or annoyed and unable to concentrate on the topic of the day until you do something to take the heat out of the situation. Here are some things that have worked for us:

- **Yawning** – ignoring it at first (it's not so unusual, after all) but if it becomes noticeable, asking the whole group if it's stuffy, would they like a window open? Perhaps looking at the yawner as you speak. Calling an early break and asking the person if they are tired – it is always possible they feel unwell or are on medication, and can tell you what they need, or just ask you to ignore it. If they are bored, hopefully they will tell you in an assertive way and you can ask them what would make the session more interesting.

- **Falling asleep** – an extreme version of yawning which can be dealt with in similar ways, except that you need to deal with it as soon as you notice by calling a break and agreeing with the individual how to address it, including how to explain it to the rest of the group.

- **Tears** – perhaps it is not surprising how upset people can become when you address topics that are not usually discussed openly – unemployment, redundancy, lack of qualifications, career goals, confidence and assertiveness. All these could awaken feelings of failure, disappointment and loss. If we think this could be an issue, we might prepare them at the start with our "How are you today?" ice breaker (see Part Three) or describe Elizabeth Kubler-Ross's change curve (Kubler-Ross, 1997). This gives them permission to have strong feelings by showing how normal it is – then when it happens, everyone is prepared and more able to cope with it. When it happens in the session, you need to protect the individual. You might either call an early break or give the rest of the group a task, so that you can have a quiet word with the person and find out how they want to handle it.

- Some will tell you the reason for their tears. One person had heard that very morning that her husband was to be made redundant, had tried to carry on as normal, but suddenly felt overwhelmed by panic and needed time to recover; another had very recently learned his wife wanted to leave him – he'd thought that attending the group session was what he needed to help him focus on the future, but it proved too much. Some prefer to remain in the room and join in again as soon as they have recovered; others want to withdraw for a few minutes, then return – you might allocate someone sympathetic to sit beside them; others realise that now is the wrong time for them to participate in group activity and decide to leave.

- **Tantrums** can often be one person's way of expressing what another expresses with tears. Some people will not be able to articulate what has upset them – in one Return to Work group a member who was trying to carry on as long as possible with a progressive illness suddenly stormed out and did not attend the next week's session. Only on phoning to ask how she was did we learn from her mother that the activity we gave the group – cutting out shapes to make a card sort – had brought it home to her that she could no longer manipulate scissors. You cannot ignore the outburst – deal with it by remaining calm yourself, showing that although it is unfortunate, you can deal with it. Then make some kind of statement to the group telling them what you intend to do – *"Let's take five minutes"* or *"Can you please get on with your CV's, I'll be back in five minutes"* while you follow the person out and have a quiet word with them.

- A tantrum directed at someone else (displaced anger?) is something you have to deal with immediately. This is Horace turning horrible and you must calmly and confidently describe the offending behaviour, say why it is unacceptable and ask him to stop now. If it is directed at you, you might also decide to empathise *"I can see that you feel angry/upset/it's unfair, but...."*. If it's directed at another group member – or at people like them, eg: *"it's all because of them..."* – then empathising will appear to collude with the attack so you need to avoid it and just say the aggressive behaviour has to stop, now.

By now, you may be feeling like investing in a suit of armour to protect you from these characters, or running for the hills. Please be reassured, the vast majority of participants will want to enjoy and learn from your session, making your work rewarding and satisfying. When things do go wrong, it is wonderful how often the rest of the group will rally to support you and each other. Surviving a difficult experience will create a really strong bond and sense of group identity. When things go right, as they usually do, everyone learns from each other and comes away with a sense of wellbeing and excitement, ready to tackle the challenges they have set themselves.

Group Dynamics

We have looked at some of the individuals you may come across and suggested ways to help them join in your group without disrupting it. While a group is made of individuals it is also true that a group can take on a life and personality of its own. Go into a school classroom or watch an angry crowd on TV and you see that the same person can behave very differently in a group than they would if you met them one to one.

Trainee managers learn about Forming, Storming, Norming and Performing (Tuckman, 1965, 1975) to help them build and lead their teams. This group life cycle theory reminds us how people feel when they join a group and how their feelings can affect their behaviour.

Forming

When people get together for the first time they are likely to be:

- Keen to participate
- Anxious about the new experience
- Cautious in how they interact - polite
- Not sure what to expect

At this stage they need:

- Friendly support to get to know others and feel they belong
- Information about goals and tasks
- Direction from the leader (that's you!)

Storming

As they start to relax they can be less cautious and start to show their real feelings. These feelings may be:

- Disappointment, frustration – this is not what I expected

- Negative reaction to leader or other people – I don't like him
- Confusion about what is going on
- Feeling incompetent, inadequate
- Demoralised, unmotivated, unproductive

At this stage they need:

- Encouragement to express their dissatisfactions: use your one to one skills – listening, empathy, and summarising – to show you value them and to explain their feelings to the rest of the group
- Support in giving and receiving negative information
- Negotiation – be prepared to adapt your aims and objectives
- To move towards becoming less dependent on the leader
- To take on a problem-solving mentality – tasks to work on
- Coaching in the skills the need to do the tasks

Norming

By going through the storming with your skilful facilitation, all their fears and frustrations are out in the open, you may have re-negotiated and clarified, and people are now ready to accept compromises – this group reaches agreement on how things are going to work. You will recognise you have reached this stage when:

- People work better together, understanding and appreciating each other
- A group identity – "we…"
- Increase in morale
- They put more effort put into the tasks
- There may be too much agreement for fear of losing the group spirit

Your role now is to start letting go, becoming less directive:

- Stand back and let them get on with tasks, allowing them to make mistakes so that they can learn from them
- Show you believe in each person's ability to carry out tasks

- Encourage them to challenge and express differences of opinion – in an appropriately assertive way, still respecting each other

Performing

This stage may be more relevant to work teams than learning groups but you will know you have helped create a really effective group when:

- People can work equally well independently, in sub-groups or as a whole group
- You see they are learning what you intended them to learn

Now your role is:

- Hands-off, stand back and let them get on with it
- Keep in mind the overall aims and objectives and the planned timing, to make sure they remain focused
- Monitor to watch out for any signs of a return to the storming stage – this may happen if new members join or if circumstances change
- Celebrate success in achieving goals and sub goals

Adjourning

Tuckman added this fifth stage later, and it is more relevant to learning sessions or project work than to ongoing work groups. He probably chose the term Adjourning because it rhymes (kind of) with the first four stages – in essence it is about closing or ending. You will know the importance of ending from your one to one work, especially if you work with people over a period of time. Even if your group is only meeting once, at the end they may feel:

- Sad at the loss of something good
- Unsure what they have achieved
- Flat, now there's no longer a goal to work towards

- Anxious about what to do next

Now they need you to:

- Become more directive again and provide leadership
- Evaluate what they have achieved – the task and the personal growth
- Help them to understand and accept their feelings by expressing them and saying it is normal
- Allow time for planning next steps
- Arrange a celebration and say good-bye – a game, a party, whatever is appropriate for the group. You do not need to be directive here – most groups love to organise this bit themselves.

A Final Word

We have reached the Adjourning stage of "The Groupwork Toolkit". We hope you have enjoyed it and found it helpful. There may be times when you stormed – too much theory; not enough depth; it didn't quite match with your own experience; you wanted more on a particular topic; you could tell more lurid *Danger!* stories. On the other hand, perhaps it has helped you overcome your fears, make practical plans and go on to really perform – delivering excellent groupwork and loving every minute of it.

Whatever your reaction, please don't keep it to yourself. We really value your feedback so please – phone us, email us, even write a review in your journal, blog or social/professional networking site. Keep in touch!

Your Next Step – Further Development

If you want to follow up any of the ideas you have read here, you can read more about them or join a taught course to help you develop your skills. There are also a few websites where you can seek out materials and resources.

Books

There are many books on the theory and/or practice of how to teach. We just include here a few of those we have either found useful ourselves or had recommended to us. Some are also included in the Bibliography, which also lists books and articles explaining some of the learning theories we mention in Part Two.

Adults Learning by Jenny Rogers (5th ed. 2007) published by Open University Press/McGraw Hill Education. Jenny is an extremely experienced trainer, tutor and coach, and provides an empathetic insight the needs of adult learners, as well as lots of practical and useable ideas for the whole process from planning through to delivering the session and evaluating it.

The Perfect Presentation by Andrew Leigh and Michael Maynard (2003) published by Random House Business Books. Although initially written pre-PowerPoint days, this neat little book is divided into short, snappy chapters focusing on how to get your mindset and behaviour right, to make your presentation interesting, lively and persuasive.

Adult Learning, Adult Teaching by J.W.Daines, Carolyn Daines and Brian Graham (4th ed. 2006) published by Welsh Academic Press. Lots of practical, useable ideas.

Getting on Brilliantly by Annette Zera and Susan Murray, (2004) published by NIACE. More a workbook, with price to match (£65 – perhaps your employer will buy it as a training resource?) provides a toolkit of strategies to help people work better together both in meetings and in learning groups with "difficult members".

The One to One Toolkit by Julie Cooper and Ann Reynolds, (2008), published by Careertrain Publishing, www.careertrain.net. We have referred to a number of techniques and resources that we first mentioned in this book, which focuses in more depth on the subject matter – Information Advice and Guidance – that will be the focus of many of your group sessions.

Courses

Teaching in the Lifelong Learning Sector

This group of programmes has been developed over the last few years to upskill everyone who teaches people aged 16 and over. To teach people aged 16+ in a publicly funded institution it is becoming essential to have the first level qualification, Preparing to Teach in the Lifelong Learning Sector.

PTLLS – Preparing to Teach in the Lifelong Learning Sector
You will find this course at most further education colleges, typically attending one three-hour session a week over one term, although many colleges offer a range of attendance modes. It is available at level 3, or taught in more depth at level 4. You will learn to plan and deliver a learning session, choose appropriate resources, use a range of methods, manage behaviour and provide feedback, as well as how to reflect on your practice and ensure you work inclusively in keeping with equality and diversity principles. You have to plan and deliver a very short "microteach" session. Successful assessment will qualify you for the Award in PTLLS. Some private providers offer a 'fast track' version. You can progress to the ...

CTLLS – Certificate in Teaching in the Lifelong Learning Sector which grants "associate teacher" status. This qualification consolidates the skills you learned on the PTLLS, taking them to greater depth, so that you will be able to design a scheme of work for a complete programme of planned sessions to meet the needs of a curriculum and of individual learners. You will learn to assess learners' work. Most further education colleges offer this over one year, often as a weekly three-hour session. Those really intending to make a career in teaching can develop further with the Diploma in Teaching in the Lifelong Learning Sector.

S/NVQs in Learning and Development

These qualifications are often used by people working in human resources and development roles in the workplace. They include units of study focusing on planning and delivering learning, including developing learning sessions, enabling group learning, making presentations, giving demonstrations and instruction and coaching.

S/NVQs in Advice and Guidance

These qualifications offer a wide choice of optional units at levels 3 and 4 that include the facilitation of learning in groups and a "borrowed" unit from the Learning and Development S/NVQ about enabling learning through demonstration and instruction.

Two things about S/NVQs

As you may already know, S/NVQs are assessment programmes designed to accredit you with a qualification rather than taught courses. Although some providers might offer a programme of taught sessions to help you gain relevant knowledge and develop skills, this may not be the case, so we would suggest you check that the programme you are considering will meet your needs.

Currently in 2010, many S/NVQs are being replaced with qualifications that will fit into the QCF credit framework. The S/NVQ in Advice and Guidance is not expected to take new registrations after the end of 2010, although those already registered will be able to gain certification up to 2013. The qualifications will remain available until the Diplomas that are currently being designed are available to replace them.

CIPD Certificate in Learning & Development Practice (CLDP)

The Chartered Institute of Personnel and Development (CIPD) who accredit this course describe it as using a highly practical approach, designed to provide an in-depth and thorough grounding in the training cycle and the fundamentals of learning and development. It is of equivalent level to NVQ/SVQ 3, and is available as a modular or fast track programme.

NOCN qualifications in Information, Advice or Guidance

The Level 3 Certificate in Information, Advice or Guidance includes an optional unit "Information, Advice or Guidance work with Groups". This qualification will take no more new registrations after the end of 2010, although we hope that a revised qualification will succeed it.

Qualification/Diploma in Career Guidance

This well established postgraduate course is available in 11 universities across the UK, together with the Qualification in Career Guidance and Development available at 2 universities in Scotland. It combines practical training with academic study and prepares you for adviser roles in Careers Services, Connexions and a range of other support agencies and educational establishments. The main focus of its practical skills training is on one to one advice and guidance, but the qualification, awarded by the Institute of Career Guidance, also includes training and assessment in working with groups.

Other Training Opportunities

Many training companies offer non accredited Train the Trainer programmes, which are usually run over two days and can give you a basic grounding in groupwork skills. Also look out for training courses in facilitation and presentation skills.

IT Training – for Better Materials and Presentations

Depending on your skill levels, you might decide to enhance your Word Processing and PowerPoint competence. ECDL or learndirect courses, or special one-off short courses at local Adult and Community Learning centres, could be worth the investment, if only to mix with other people and pick up their design ideas.

Finding a Provider

It is one thing to know that a qualification exists, quite another to find a provider that offers it.

You could approach the local colleges in your area or use the "Find a Course" tab currently available on www.careersadvice.direct.gov.uk.

A full list of institutions offering the Qualification in Career Guidance courses is available on www.icg-uk.org.

For the PTLLS, S/NVQ and NOCN courses, you could approach the awarding bodies who should be able to tell you which institutions are offering their qualification: particularly approach the following who currently offer qualifications in Advice and Guidance and/or Teaching in the Lifelong Learning Sector.

www.cityandguilds.com

www.edexcel.com

www.ediplc.com

www.ncfe.org.uk

www.nocn.org.uk

www.ocr.org.uk

www.open.ac.uk.ouab

www.sqa.org.uk

also...

www.cipd.org.uk offers the Learning and Development NVQ and the CLDP.

Websites

Here we list a few websites that develop some of the themes in the book. They offer resources for you to use in your group sessions. You will find further resources, specifically to use in IAG guidance work, listed in the One to One Toolkit.

http://www.thetrainingshop.co.uk Lots of "executive toys", fun stationery and other props, sweets and treats to lighten up your session – it even has a set of coloured cotton hats for the "Six Hats" exercise – plus things that make noises (eg: a bell for calling time) and ideas for games and ice breakers.

http://www.learningandteaching.info for those who enjoy theory – this site written by an enthusiastic teacher trainer has some practical ideas too, and is presented in a light-hearted, colourful style.

http://www.businessballs.com has sections on teambuilding, self development and amusement/stress relief. It contains both theory and ideas for running activities. Check out the evaluation section, and also the three stage behavioural assessment, which can be adapted to be a useful 'before and after' measure.

http://www.teachers.tv is aimed at those working in schools, although the PSHE/Careers page may have some useful resources to incorporate into your presentation.

http://www.jumpcutuk.com Jumpcut Ltd is a company producing and selling reasonably priced DVDs and videos on how to job search – CV writing, interview techniques, phoning employers.

We apologise for all the websites and resources we haven't mentioned here. If you find something good, make sure you share it with your colleagues, and we'd be happy to hear about it too!

Bibliography

ANDERSON, L W, & KRATHWOHL D R (eds.), 2001, *A Taxonomy for Learning, Teaching, and Assessing: A Revision of Bloom's Taxonomy of Educational Objectives.* New York: Longman

BANDURA, Albert, 1977, *Social Learning Theory.* New Jersey: Prentice Hall

BEDFORD, Tol, 1982, *Vocational Guidance Interviews Explored.* London: Careers Service Branch, Department of Employment.

BINET, Alfred, & SIMON, Theophile, 1916, *The development of intelligence in children*. Baltimore: Williams & Wilkins. (Reprinted 1973, New York: Arno Press; 1983, Salem, NH: Ayer Company).

BLOOM, B S (ed.), 1956, *Taxonomy of Educational Objectives, the classification of educational goals – Handbook I: Cognitive Domain.* New York: McKay

COOPER, Julie & REYNOLDS, Ann, 2008, *The One to One Toolkit.* Peterborough: Careertrain Publishing

DAVE, R H, 1975, in *Developing and Writing Behavioural Objectives* (R J Armstrong, ed.): Educational Innovators Press

GAGNÉ, Robert, 1965, *The Conditions of Learning (4th ed.).* New York: Holt, Rinehart & Winston

GARDNER, Howard, 1983, *Frames of Mind: The Theory of Multiple Intelligences.* New York: Basic

GREGORC, Anthony F, 1982, *An Adult's Guide to Style.* Maynard, Massachusetts: Gabriel Systems, Inc.

GUILFORD, J P, 1967, *The Nature of Human Intelligence*. New York: McGraw-Hill

HONEY, Peter & MUMFORD, Alan, 1992, *The Manual of Learning Styles*. Maidenhead: Peter Honey Publications Ltd

HOPSON, Barry & SCALLY, Mike, 1999, *Build Your Own Rainbow: a lifeskills workbook for career and life management*. Cirencester, UK: Management Books 2000 Ltd

INSTONE, Ayd, *The Goal Chasm* (last accessed 14-06-2010) http://www.aydinstone.com/tools-goalchasm.html

KNOWLES, Malcolm, 1984, *The Adult Learner: A Neglected Species (3rd Ed.)*. Houston, Texas: Gulf Publishing

KOLB, David A, 1985, *Experiential Learning: experience as the source of learning and development.* Englewood Cliffs, NJ, USA: Prentice-Hall

KUBLER-ROSS, Elisabeth, 1997 reprint, *On Death and Dying.* New York: Scribner.

LEIGH, Andrew & MAYNARD, Michael, 2003, *The Perfect Presentation.* London: Random House Business Books

MASLOW, Abraham Harold, 1987, *Motivation and Personality*, 3rd (revised) edition. New York: Harper and Row.

McLEOD, Angus, 2003, *Performance Coaching.* Carmarthen, Wales: Crown House Publishing Ltd.

PAVLOV, Ivan P, 1927, *Conditioned Reflexes: An Investigation of the Physiological Activity of the Cerebral Cortex. Translated and Edited by G. V. Anrep*. London: Oxford University Press

PIAGET, Jean, 1937, *The Construction of Reality in the Child. Translated 1954, Reprinted 2002,* Abingdon: Routledge

ROGERS, Jenny, 2007, *Adults Learning* (5th ed) Maidenhead: Open University Press / McGraw Hill

TUCKMAN, Bruce W, 1965, *Developmental sequence in small groups*, in Psychological Bulletin, 63, 384-399

TUCKMAN, Bruce W & JENSEN, Mary Ann C. (1977). 'Stages of small group development revisited', *Group and Organizational Studies*, 2, 419- 427

Index